IMAGES OF WAR
PRELUDE TO WAR: THE RAF, 1936–1939

RARE PHOTOGRAPHS FROM WARTIME ARCHIVES

CW00821904

IMAGES OF WAR
PRELUDE TO WAR: THE RAF, 1936–1939

RARE PHOTOGRAPHS FROM WARTIME ARCHIVES

MARTIN DERRY

AIR WORLD

First published in Great Britain in 2020 by
PEN & SWORD AIR WORLD
An imprint of
Pen & Sword Books Ltd
Yorkshire – Philadelphia

Copyright © Martin Derry 2020

ISBN 978 1 52675 482 0

The right of Martin Derry to be identified as Author of this work has been asserted
by him in accordance with the Copyright, Designs and Patents Act 1988.

A CIP catalogue record for this book is
available from the British Library.

All rights reserved. No part of this book may be reproduced or transmitted in any
form or by any means, electronic or mechanical including photocopying, recording
or by any information storage and retrieval system, without permission from the
Publisher in writing.

Printed and bound in the UK by CPI Group (UK) Ltd,
Croydon, CR0 4YY

Pen & Sword Books Limited incorporates the imprints of Atlas, Archaeology, Aviation,
Discovery, Family History, Fiction, History, Maritime, Military, Military Classics, Politics,
Select, Transport, True Crime, Air World, Frontline Publishing, Leo Cooper, Remember
When, Seaforth Publishing, The Praetorian Press, Wharncliffe Local History, Wharncliffe
Transport, Wharncliffe True Crime and White Owl.

For a complete list of Pen & Sword titles please contact

PEN & SWORD BOOKS LIMITED
47 Church Street, Barnsley, South Yorkshire, S70 2AS, England
E-mail: enquiries@pen-and-sword.co.uk
Website: www.pen-and-sword.co.uk

Or

PEN AND SWORD BOOKS
1950 Lawrence Rd, Havertown, PA 19083, USA
E-mail: Uspen-and-sword@casematepublishers.com
Website: www.penandswordbooks.com

Contents

Acknowledgements   vi

Abbreviations   vii

Introduction   viii

Chapter 1: The Fighters   1

Chapter 2: The Bombers   50

Chapter 3: The Searchers: Maritime Patrol   105

Chapter 4: General-Purpose, Army Co-Operation and Miscellaneous Duties   132

Chapter 5: Waiting in the Wings: The New Order(s)   159

Acknowledgements

I would like to take this opportunity to acknowledge the generosity of the following individuals in providing so many of the photographs included in this volume, namely: Tony Buttler, Tony O'Toole, Mike Smith (Newark Air Museum) and Carl Vincent. Their respective contributions are, as ever, much appreciated.

Unless otherwise indicated, photographs are supplied by or via the author.

Abbreviations

AACU	Anti-Aircraft Co-operation Unit
A&AEE	Aeroplane & Armament Experimental Establishment
AAF	Auxiliary Air Force
AOS	Air Observers School
ATS	Advanced Training Squadron
B&GS	Bombing & Gunnery School
CSU	Constant Speed Unit
FBTS	Flying Boat Training Squadron
FTS	Flying Training School
GDGS	Group Defence Gunners School
GP	General-Purpose (aircraft)
LRDU/LRDF	Long Range Development Unit (also known as Long Range Development Flight)
MAEE	Marine Aircraft Experimental Establishment
MU	Maintenance Unit
OTU	Operational Training Unit
PR	Photographic Reconnaissance/Photo-Reconnaissance
RAAF	Royal Australian Air Force
RAE	Royal Aircraft Establishment
RCAF	Royal Canadian Air Force
RNZAF	Royal New Zealand Air Force
RPG	Rounds per Gun
RPM	Rounds per Minute
RPM	Revolutions per Minute
SAAF	South African Air Force
SOC	Struck Off Charge
STS	Seaplane Training Squadron

Introduction

Setting the Scene

Following the German invasion of Poland on 1 September 1939, Britain and France declared war against Germany two days later; one year after the Munich crisis of late September 1938. Considered retrospectively, it is probably useful to regard the crisis as a 'wake-up' call to the British people, despite Neville Chamberlain's speech following his return from Munich in which he advised '…I believe it is peace for our time. Go home and get a nice quiet sleep.' In reality, war was already inevitable.

Chamberlain was referring to an agreement whereby the British, French, Italian and German leaders (Chamberlain, Daladier, Mussolini and Hitler respectively) had arrived at a political 'understanding' in which the Sudetenland, a fortified region of Czechoslovakia, was to be ceded to Nazi Germany. This agreement, reached in conference on 29 September 1938 and termed the Munich Agreement, was achieved without Czech government representatives being present, their request to attend having been refused by Hitler.

Chamberlain was a committed supporter of appeasement towards Hitler, a policy both he and Daladier believed necessary to avert a European war and ensure a lasting peace. Did Chamberlain truly believe he had indeed bought a lasting peace? Probably, at least initially, but when in March 1939, Hitler annexed the remaining Czech lands of Bohemia and Moravia, and Slovakia became a German puppet state, even Chamberlain accepted that war was inevitable.

Importantly and despite the political rhetoric, Chamberlain's 'Peace for our time' did buy actual time; eleven months as it turned out, a period that allowed Britain's armed forces to *further* accelerate their preparations for the inevitable war. Why 'further accelerate'? Because the need to improve and expand Britain's armed forces didn't commence as a result of Czechoslovakia's dismemberment, this had already commenced in 1934.

Munich was one in a long sequence of events leading inexorably to war; a war that Winston Churchill always believed was simply a continuation of the First World War. That Germany had been ruined financially and politically by the Great War is undeniable, but because much of the country was left unoccupied by allied forces it remained undefeated in the eyes of most Germans. The terms of the 1919 Versailles Treaty caused great bitterness among the populace which quickly allowed extremist political parties to flourish and survive in a republic largely devoid of a stable political system. During the 1920s several extreme political factions grew, destabilizing then eradicating whatever remained of a balanced political system. Ultimately, only the most ruthless succeeded, and it scarcely needs recording that the most ruthless of them all was the Nazi Party under Adolf Hitler.

From the outset, Hitler strove to increase the power of all arms of the German military with increasingly large rearmament programmes in contravention of the 1925 Treaty of Locarno. This in turn emphasized, in Germany's case, the restrictions imposed at Versailles concerning the size of the land and sea forces permitted to them and which prohibited a German military air force. The Locarno Treaty also outlawed any acts of aggression between the signatories, of which Germany was one. Hitler's new measures went hand-in-hand with his avowed intent to incorporate all of Europe's Teutonic peoples into a Greater Germany.

In March 1935 Hitler repudiated the Versailles Treaty; Britain and France, lacking both will and determination, did nothing. In 1936, Hitler's forces entered and re-militarized the Rhineland, a buffer zone between Germany and France established after the Great War, and again not a finger was lifted against him beyond limp diplomatic protests. Hitler was emboldened. Austria, a country rich in iron-ore deposits, was taken into Hitler's orbit in March 1938. Following this, as related, he demanded and received the Czech Sudetenland later in 1938, annexed the rest of the country along with the Lithuanian port of Memel in March 1939, and culminated in invading Poland on 1 September 1939. He ignored all protestations from other nations and, specifically, warnings from Britain and France that his actions would lead to war.

Although this book is concerned primarily with the RAF at home during the last years of peace in Europe, it is important to recall that Britain still had a responsibility to defend its Empire and dominions. At a time of Nazi ascendency, with all its implications, the British government was also concerned with the growing threat from Fascist Italy as it carved a new empire for itself in the Mediterranean and Horn of Africa, leading to territorial acquisitions which would later threaten Britain's lines of communication to India and beyond. Mussolini, like Hitler, had also recognized an international unwillingness to confront acts of military aggression. Meanwhile, Imperial Japan continued to pursue its belligerent interests far beyond its borders and those areas of mainland China already subjugated in Japan's quest for regional domination and natural resources. Thus Japan also presented a major concern to Britain, particularly the defence of Australia, New Zealand, Malaya, Singapore and Hong Kong.

The Royal Air Force had reached its nadir in terms of manpower and equipment in the years immediately following the Great War and by 1923 the Home Defence programme had recognized that Britain's air defences needed to be expanded in order to offer a credible level of offensive and defensive security. The optimum figure decided upon was for fifty-two home-based squadrons: seventeen fighter and thirty-five bomber. (Nine years later this 'expansion' had risen to just 42 squadrons with 490 aircraft, one-third of which were allocated to non-regular and cadre units.)

By the time of the League of Nation's Disarmament Conference on 2 February 1932, the British government's position (or policy of despair) was that if Britain itself did not re-arm, then the other nations represented at the conference might follow its example, both on moral grounds and out of respect for the country's own self-imposed immolation. None did.

As for air forces specifically, Britain's ranking in the world front-line air-strength league fell to fifth place behind those of France, the USSR, the USA and Italy. Because of the government's policy, the fifty-two-squadron scheme of 1923 was halted and didn't reach its intended total. The RAF remained under-strength. Adding to the nation's woes was the fact that Britain was in the midst of a deep financial crisis; consequently its lack of military expansion was in part explained by economic and not just political or pacifist considerations alone, although the same financial crisis also gripped Europe and the USA!

Britain, along with other nations, gained knowledge of Germany's military resurgence from early 1934. Although concerns were expressed internationally as Germany began to expand its land and maritime forces, particular anxieties emerged as knowledge filtered through of the emergence of a new German air force, the Luftwaffe (officially created on 26 February 1935), and its future implications. In Britain, despite ongoing financial concerns and general pacifist convictions, the news caused the government to re-examine its defence policies in general and the parlous state of the RAF in particular. In May 1934 the Cabinet was moved to state '… the accumulated evidence that Germany has started to rearm in earnest …' required the government to realize '…it would be unsafe to delay the initiation of steps to provide for the safety of the country.' In retrospect it may be said that Britain's initial, sometimes faltering, rearmament programme for all three services dates from this time. More specifically, from the RAF's perspective, the MP Stanley Baldwin (prime minister from 7 June 1935 to 28 May 1937), stated to the *Manchester Guardian* on 12 June 1934: 'We could simply not avoid increasing our air force.' He specified that the rise of a new Germany had altered for the worse the situation in Europe and that the government could not take risks '…it was the trustee for the people of the country, and it had got to have an adequate means of defence, as far as those could be provided.' In mid-1934, these comments may be seen to indicate a need for more bombing aircraft.

Accordingly, in July 1934, Scheme 'A' was approved by the Cabinet. This was the first in a series of alphabetically-listed aircraft expansion schemes designed firstly to enable Britain to overtake the German lead in military aircraft construction (already believed to be numerically superior to the RAF), and secondly to dissuade Hitler from any hostile acts or policies towards Britain. By 1935 the stated intention was to demonstrate Britain's ability to out-build Germany 'keel for keel' as it was then phrased, bringing with it a distant echo of the pre-First World War naval arms race when both countries had sought to build dreadnoughts, the arbiters of power before the advent of military aviation.

That the expansion schemes failed in their strictest sense – i.e. they neither overtook the Luftwaffe's lead nor deterred Hitler from his hostile intent – is now obvious, but they did allow the RAF to become at least adequately prepared for war in 1939 and certainly to a far greater extent than it was in September 1938. Churchill had summed up the reality even earlier in 1937 by stating '…the paramount fact remained that the Germans had the lead of us in the air, and also over the whole field of munitions production.' He continued 'It was no longer in our power to forestall Hitler or to regain air parity. Nothing could now prevent the German Army and the German Air Force from becoming the strongest in Europe…we could only improve our position. We could not cure it.'

Churchill's understanding of the extent of Hitler's rearmament was not based solely upon his own knowledge or reports circulated in the press; he had other sources. In early 1936 he had apparently been privy to information from a highly-placed government official (whose identity was not divulged) that Germany was to spend the equivalent of '£1,000 million pounds sterling' during the year on armaments; a staggering sum of money in 1936, representing approximately half of their combined spend for 1933, 1934 and 1935. That this sum later proved to be exaggerated is irrelevant; what mattered at the time was the perception that it was true. These figures caused a stir when Churchill revealed them in the House of Commons later in the year to the then Chancellor of the Exchequer, Neville Chamberlain. Chamberlain (prime minister from 28 May 1937) did not dispute the figures, but entertained an element of doubt and caution with regard to them. Suffice to say Churchill's words, plus those of other like-minded politicians and senior RAF officers, did have an impact in convincing the Treasury to begin loosening its purse-strings, despite subsequent allegations that they (meaning Churchill mostly) were being overly dramatic and pessimistic with regard to the Luftwaffe's true strength!

Space precludes an elaborate explanation of the RAF's expansion programme from 1934 to 1939 or the practical and political methods by which it was achieved; all have been addressed by historians and academics far better qualified than this author to explain such matters. That said, attention must be drawn to two critical changes in policy made during the years of RAF expansion:

1) Following WWI, Britain and other nations followed an accepted doctrine espousing the dominance in future wars of the bomber and its ability, given sufficient numbers, to always defeat the aerial defences of the target country – often summed up by repeating Prime Minister Baldwin's reluctant assertion that '…the bomber will always get through'. This led to a larger proportion of financial resources being directed toward the bomber as opposed to defending fighters at a time when technology seemed unable to provide a meaningful performance advantage to the fighter over contemporary light bombers that could often outpace the interceptors. Yet by 1936 the bombers' seemingly unassailable position looked set to be usurped as a new era of high-performance, low-wing monoplane fighter designs was slowly ushered in.

   Lessons were also gleaned during the Spanish Civil War which indicated, Guernica notwithstanding (April 1937), that the effect of bombing cities did not have quite the apocalyptic effect predicted by authors over the previous decade or so. For the cost-conscious British Government this permitted a significant change in policy: instead of fielding an armada of expensive, multi-seat, multi-engined bombers with which to deter an enemy, would it not be better to adopt a defensive policy instead? Consequently, in 1937, the Minister for the Co-ordination of Defence – Sir Thomas Inskip – was appointed to examine the situation. In essence, he reoriented British air policy and argued that the RAF's principal role was to defend Great Britain's airspace whilst retaining a viable fleet of bombers should war break out. In Inskip's words the role of the RAF lay not in achieving '…an early knock-out blow, but to prevent the Germans from knocking us out'. In short, financially, Britain was unable to afford a continual aerial arms race with Germany, a race in which Britain already believed itself to be a lot further behind the rest of the field than it actually was. Ergo, an air force comprising more fighters and fewer bombers was a cheaper option.

2) In mid-July 1936 the RAF reorganized itself by eliminating its previous geographically-based fighting, bombing and coastal areas and instead formed three new commands based on function rather than location. These became respectively: Fighter Command, Bomber Command and Coastal Command and were created under Expansion Scheme 'F' which

had been approved five months earlier and allowed for a doubling in size of the RAF by March 1939. (For clarity, the RAF's existing army co-operation units were placed within the purview of Fighter Command for administrative purposes only until, in December 1940, RAF Army Co-Operation Command was created.)

Returning to the political and financial questions of the day, 1936 saw the increased promise of modern high-performance monoplane fighters becoming available in the near future with the merest hint that a new radio direction-finding device was being developed. Could the latter, combined with the new fighters, eventually point to an entirely new system of air defence?

Within a fairly short period of time, a progressive chain of strange wooden towers extended along much of the eastern and southern coasts of Britain which would soon become 'force multipliers' in the defence of the nation when its new fighters, and even newer radar, were tested to their utmost during the Battle of Britain in 1940. Even today, that air defence system still stands as one of the few instances in modern military history in which a defensive system was actually used for the purpose for which it was intended.

To help appreciate the extent of RAF pre-war expansion, it is hoped that the aircraft production list below might be of benefit, although the figures should be viewed guardedly as they are unlikely to be absolutely precise. They show the quantities of aircraft procured by the Air Ministry (the government department responsible for managing RAF affairs from 1918 to 1964, headed by the Secretary of State for Air) which include training, transport and Fleet Air Arm types as well. (The Admiralty didn't regain full control of the FAA until May 1939.)[*] It is uncertain if aircraft purchased by Britain from the USA in 1938/39 are included or not; i.e. the North American Harvard and Lockheed Hudson.

1934: Total production 1,110 [549] (Figures in brackets show quantities procured for front-line duty)
1935: Total production 901 [497]
1936: Total production 1,830 [868]
1937: Total production 2,230 [1,301]
1938: Total production 2,831 [1,401]
1939: Total production 7,940 [3,730] (Presumably for the whole of 1939!)

These figures suggest that Britain obtained approximately 16,842 aircraft for military use from 1934 to 1939, of which 8,346 were front-line types. By comparison the Luftwaffe is believed to have received approximately 29,400 military aircraft in the same period, of which perhaps 14,900 were combat aircraft.

---

[*] Until the Admiralty regained full control, the Fleet Air Arm remained under the auspices of the RAF thus, as an entity in its own right, the FAA remains outside the scope of this book. It is hoped that a later volume will correct this omission.

Chapter One

The Fighters

By September 1938, RAF Fighter Command had begun to receive monoplane fighters and was feeling its way towards operational efficiency, with five squadrons equipped or equipping with Hawker Hurricanes and one other receiving Supermarine Spitfires in lieu of Gloster Gauntlets. However, not all were as yet operational and few if any reserves existed. Otherwise Britain's fighter defences relied upon an all-biplane force comprising nine or ten squadrons of Gauntlets, six with Gloster Gladiators, seven or eight with Hawker Demons and three with Hawker Furies, all of which were utterly outflown by Bristol Blenheim bombers during a series of air exercises held a year earlier in 1937.

Thus the eleven months after Munich proved as valuable to Fighter Command as it did to the rest of the RAF, for which a lot more was required beyond simply creating more and more front-line squadrons: existing units had to be sustained and replenished, increasing numbers of pilots and ground crew had to be trained, and substantial material reserves established. Even so, it would be wrong to assume that by 3 September 1939 all of the biplane fighters had been swept away as at least four Gladiator squadrons still remained, as indeed did two others which still fielded Gauntlets.

By autumn of 1939, the balance of numbers had swung sharply in favour of the Hurricane and Spitfire, yet during October and November 1939, as expansion continued, three home-based fighter squadrons either re-formed or were re-equipped with Gladiators.

It is perhaps worth noting that the term Fighter Command referred to the RAF's Regular fighter units which c mid-1939 consisted of twenty-five squadrons (albeit numbers would fluctuate as squadrons reformed or re-equipped). In addition, fourteen or so Auxiliary[*] fighter squadrons existed at that time, although many were still awaiting the arrival of modern fighters, two of whom (615 and 616 Squadrons) were still operating Gauntlets on 3 September 1939. From a total of thirty-nine squadrons, it was agreed that four Hurricane squadrons, later adjusted to six fighter squadrons (and later still more) would accompany British ground forces in France. Furthermore, it was decided they must also provide for the protection of Scapa Flow and yet more squadrons were to be tasked with protecting coastal convoys.

---

[*] Commencing with 602 Squadron in September 1925, the RAF's Regular squadrons were gradually augmented by regionally-based Auxiliary Air Force squadrons. AAF units were numbered 600 to 605 and 607 to 616 Squadrons. 616 Squadron was initiated on 1 November 1938 following the renumbering of 503 Squadron, while 613 became the last pre-war AAF unit to form in March 1939. Commencing with 502 Squadron on 15 May 1925, five Special Reserve units were formed. 500 to 504 Squadrons were bomber units and remained so until transferred to the AAF in 1936 (1937 in 502's case).

Just qualifying for inclusion in this account, the Bristol Bulldog had first entered service in 1929 when it began to replace the Gloster Gamecock and later the Armstrong Whitworth Siskin. By the early to mid-1930s Bulldogs formed the backbone of Britain's fighter defences. Ten RAF squadrons ultimately operated the type, although this total was only achieved for a brief period between October 1932 and April 1933 when 23 Squadron's remaining Bulldogs gave way to the Hawker Demon. In 1936, six squadrons were still equipped with the obsolescent Bulldog, but it was 1937 before 3 Squadron, the first squadron to operate the type, also became the last when, from March 1937, their now thoroughly obsolete mounts were replaced by the Gloster Gladiator I.

Seen here c 1936 is 32 Squadron Bulldog IIA K1606, with, appropriately, the Bristol factory's bulldog logo on the fin. By this time K1606 had been fitted retrospectively with a tail wheel in lieu of a tail skid, an improved undercarriage with broader tyres and better brakes, although its performance and armament remained unchanged with a maximum speed of 178 mph at 8,000ft and two fixed Vickers Mk III .303in machine guns with 600 rounds per gun (rpg). No. 32 Squadron exchanged its Bulldog IIAs for the Gloster Gauntlet II in July 1936, while K1606 survived to become maintenance airframe 905M on 23 November 1936.

The Hawker Fury entered service in 1931, its role being that of a fast-climbing aircraft intended to intercept enemy bombers after they left the Continent and crossed the English coastline east or south of London, leaving the more numerous but slower Bulldogs based further inland with time to gain sufficient altitude to attack the enemy before they reached the capital. The Fury was the first RAF fighter in squadron service to exceed 200 mph in level flight (207 mph at 14,000ft), giving it a comfortable edge over contemporary heavy bomber designs but much less so over the then modern Hawker Hart two-seat light bomber's maximum speed of 184 mph. Seen here in 1935, Fury I K1942 belonged to 43 Squadron which became the first squadron to receive the type in May 1931 when it replaced Siskin IIIAs at Tangmere.

In February 1932, Tangmere-based 1 Squadron relinquished its Siskins for the Fury I. Here K2040 flies line abreast with Fury Is K2043, K5673 and K2881 in 1936 when they formed 1 Squadron's aerobatic team. This photograph predates 28 August 1936, the day that K2040 hit the ground while diving onto a target and was written off as a consequence.

Black and white photography definitely has its limits where 1930s' RAF biplanes are concerned and many pitfalls await the unwary when attempting to interpret the colours and markings employed by so many units during this period. Suffice to say then, whereas the unit markings of both 1 and 25 Squadrons might appear to be identical in black and white, 1 Squadron's fuselage and upper wing bars were red and those of 25 Squadron were black.

Fury I K2900 from 1 Squadron is seen here on an unknown date carrying the individual code 'K' on the forward fuselage, hinting perhaps at 1935. Another image of K2900 coded 'K', dated 1935, does exist, albeit without national markings on the rudder! No. 1 Squadron received the Hurricane I from October 1938 and relinquished its last Furies the following month. (*Carl Vincent via Tony O'Toole*)

No. 25 Squadron was the third of the trio of Fury I squadrons intended to blunt the impact of enemy bombers that might theoretically be despatched from the direction of France or the Low Countries. To bedevil the tiny number of Fury squadrons available, their pilots filed consistent reports regarding gun stoppages or other faults with their twin Vickers machine guns at higher altitudes. Fortunately, RAF Furies were never called upon to fire their guns in anger, although a number of ex-RAF machines transferred to the South African Air Force did go into action against the Italian Air Force over East Africa in 1940 and shot down two or three Italian aircraft.

Based at Hawkinge, 25 Squadron received Fury I K2078 in January 1933 and retained it until early 1937, by which time the unit had been operating the faster Fury II since October 1936. No. 25 Squadron's motif (a hawk rising off a gauntlet) can be seen on the fin above the logo '*Feriens tego*' ('Striking, I defend').

Fury II K7275, seen prior to delivery in October 1936. The Mk II offered a small performance advantage over the Mk I in that its top speed in level flight advanced by 16 mph to 223 mph, and the time taken to reach 10,000ft improved from 4.5 minutes to 3.8, an important consideration for an interceptor. Weaponry remained the same. Of the three Fury I squadrons, just one, 25 Squadron, received the new type which it operated until October 1937.

However, in 1937 three further front-line units also received the Fury II: 41 Squadron, re-equipped at Catterick in October 1937; 73 Squadron, re-formed at Mildenhall in March 1937; and 87 Squadron, re-formed at Tangmere in March 1937.

Although obsolete by 1937, with expansion of the RAF gathering pace, the Fury, along with an entire fleet of other obsolescent types, had roles to play in the advanced training of pilots or as grounded instructional airframes needed to expand the pool of skilled ground crew.

Returning to the Fury, its greatest contribution was probably an unsung one when, late in its life, it enabled a few front-line fighter units to re-form at a critical time with others going to the Flying Training Schools' Advanced Training Squadrons for use by nascent fighter pilots. For whatever reason, it seems that the RAF's last airworthy Furies were grounded on 14 January 1940, but doubtless there would have been exceptions. (*Newark Air Museum*)

No. 25 Squadron Fury IIs led by K7270 in 1937. All were from the first Mk II production batch and all were passed to 41 Squadron later in the year except K7279, which suffered an engine failure and was written off as a result of the ensuing forced landing on 3 August 1937 near Dymchurch.

When the Hawker Hart light bomber entered RAF service in 1930, its speed and manoeuvrability were such that contemporary fighters had great difficulty intercepting it. Equally, the Hart proved to be robust, reliable and adaptable, so much so that a series of two-seat designs quickly followed, each based on the Hart, of which one became the Hawker Demon two-seat fighter.

Initially called the Hart Fighter, it received a more powerful engine than the Hart bomber, featured two fixed forward-firing Vickers machine guns instead of one and a flexible Lewis machine gun in a rear cockpit featuring a cut-down coaming to improve its arc of fire. Six examples were ordered initially, all going to Bulldog-equipped 23 Squadron in July 1931 where they formed a separate flight.

With full production under way, the fighter's name was changed to Demon in July 1932, the first of which entered RAF service in February 1933, again with 23 Squadron and replacing its Bulldogs entirely. The Demon reintroduced the two-seat fighter to RAF service, a concept made famous fifteen years earlier by the Bristol Fighter, although it was soon discovered that the much greater speed of the Demon (182 mph at 16,200ft) made it hard for the gunner to train his weapon at high speeds.

This image shows Demon K2850, coded 'L', which served 23 Squadron from May 1933 to August 1935 after which it was despatched to Malta. Upon its return and following a period in storage, K2850 went to 600 Squadron in February 1938. The fin displays the 23 Squadron motif – an eagle preying on a falcon – with the words '*semper aggressus*' ('Always on the attack') below. The unit's colours seen on the fuselage (and atop the upper wing) consisted of alternating red and blue squares.

Demon K4500 from 604 (County of Middlesex) Squadron seen in July 1936. The interlocking triangles along the fuselage (and upper wing) were red above yellow, with red and yellow segmented wheel covers. A County of Middlesex Arms motif appears on the fin. Having later served with 23 Squadron, followed by a period in storage, K4500 was allocated to 9 Bombing & Gunnery School (B&GS) in April 1940 where it served until grounded six months later. No. 604 Squadron replaced its Demons with the Blenheim Mk IF from January 1939.

Demon K5737, seen while serving with 29 Squadron in 1937/38. The black rectangles partially obscuring the serial numbers are racks for light bombs. Allocated to 9 B&GS in April 1940, it continued to fly until late October 1940 when it became maintenance airframe 2290M.

Demon K4518, belonging to 'D' Flight, 6 Squadron, as seen at Ismailia, Egypt in 1936. Due to a general threat to British interests in the Eastern Mediterranean, Palestine and Abyssinia during 1935/36, a number of Demons were despatched from Britain to locations within these regions to provide an element of air defence. Thus 'D' Flight was temporarily attached to 6 Squadron – a Hart-equipped army co-operation unit – from October 1935 to late 1936. Based near the Suez Canal, some of its aircraft were forward-based at Ramleh, Palestine. Upon returning to the UK, K4518 was issued to 64 Squadron on 1 November 1937 but stalled and crashed twenty-nine days later.

An anonymous and camouflaged 74 Squadron Demon seen at Malta in 1936. (*Tony O'Toole collection*)

Reformed in the UK on 1 September 1935 and shipped to the Mediterranean in response to the Italian invasion of Abyssinia, 74 Squadron arrived at Hal Far, Malta, ten days later where it remained for one year. Unusually for the time, 74 Squadron's Demons were camouflaged over the ensuing weeks with a multi-coloured scheme using dopes acquired locally. Here the unit's Demons display their new camouflage as well as a remarkable degree of variation in the positioning of their (single) upper mainplane roundel. (In addition to 74 Squadron, also as a result of the Abyssinian crisis, 29 and 64 Demon Squadrons were sent to Egypt to provide fighter protection, with 41 Squadron going to Aden for the same purpose.) (*Tony O'Toole collection*)

J9933, the first production Hawker Hart, was used in various tests and trials, some being dedicated to finding ways of protecting Demon rear gunners from the aircraft's slipstream. As related earlier, Demon gunners had experienced great difficulty in aiming their gun at higher speeds; i.e. anything over 130 mph (non-turret Demons could just exceed 180 mph at 16,300ft). Ultimately a solution of sorts was achieved with the development of a hydraulic turret, the FN1, produced by Nash & Thompson. (Esmonde Thompson and Archibald Frazer Nash established a company in 1929 called Nash & Thompson. They developed hydraulic gun turrets invented by Frazer Nash and marketed them using the soon-to-be familiar prefix 'FN'.) The FN1, as fitted to J9933 late in 1933, did assist gunners in improving their accuracy, but at a cost to the pilots who discovered that when rotated the turret could disturb the Demon's trim, making it harder for the pilot to sight his guns.

Sources differ as to how many Demons were built for the RAF. Excluding the six Hart Fighters, it seems likely that 232 Demons were delivered to the RAF, 126 of which were built and delivered by Hawker between 1933 and 1936, of which the last 49 received turrets at some stage. These were then supplemented by 106 Demons produced by Boulton Paul at Wolverhampton and delivered between September 1936 and early 1938, of which 34 were delivered as Turret Demons with 28 others having turrets fitted retrospectively.

A closer view of J9933's FN1 turret. As can be seen, the gunner was protected by a four-segment shield soon to be nicknamed 'lobster-back' for obvious reasons; equally obvious is the fact that the turret was not fully enclosed.

Three Boulton Paul-built Demons from 29 Squadron seen in close formation with Demon K5737 (seen earlier) leading K5736 and K5900. Strictly speaking, K5736 and K5737 were turreted Demons, while K5900 was built as a Turret Demon. No. 29 Squadron received the Blenheim IF from December 1938.

Serial numbered A1-1 to A1-64, sixty-four Demons were delivered in three batches of eighteen, plus a final one of ten aircraft, to the Royal Australian Air Force between May 1935 and May 1938. The first batch were described as 'general-purpose fighters' while those in the next two were equipped for army co-operation duties. The final ten airframes differed slightly in that dual controls and target-towing equipment were incorporated. By late 1939 most of the fifty-four survivors had been relegated to subsidiary roles, with one or two still airworthy as late as 1943.

The last of the RAF's open-cockpit fighters, the Gloster Gauntlet, was introduced into service by 19 Squadron from January (not May) 1935, when it began receiving nineteen of the twenty-four Mk Is built. The type soon proved capable of intercepting the Hart bombers that were giving the Bulldog IIA such a difficult time. Three years later, in August 1938, the unit became the first to introduce the Spitfire into RAF service. No. 19 Squadron retained its Gauntlet Is and IIs for a little longer, as pilots and ground crew transitioned from a 230 mph open-cockpit, fixed undercarriage, two-bay, two-gun biplane fighter to an eight-gun 360 mph monoplane. Their last Gauntlets left on 17 January 1939, although several Mk Is were then despatched to the Middle East for issue to 6 Squadron to augment their existing Hawker Hardys. K4092, seen wearing the unit's blue and white chequerboard markings, wasn't so fortunate: delivered on 4 March 1935, it was damaged and SOC nine months later.

The Gauntlet I was followed, unsurprisingly, by the Gauntlet II. More surprising perhaps were the quantities included in the follow-on orders, a reflection of the increasing concern by now surrounding German rearmament. Following the 1934 order for 24 Mk Is, the next order, placed in April 1935, was for 104 Gauntlet IIs to be delivered between March and August 1936, an order soon augmented by another for 100 Mk IIs to be delivered between September 1936 and February 1937.

The next RAF unit to receive the Gauntlet was 17 Squadron which began receiving Mk IIs in August 1936, with Mk II K5359 having arrived by the end of the month. K5359 remained with the unit until it crashed almost three years later in May 1939, one month prior to 17 Squadron being re-equipped with Hurricanes.

In 1936, three distinct types of role-related 'frames' began to appear on the fins of many RAF aircraft. The frames enclosed a motif which, in this instance, shows 17 Squadron's gauntlet motif set within an arrowhead - the latter defining a fighter unit. Of the other two types of frame, a grenade was used for bombers while a star denoted a reconnaissance squadron. However, at least one transport squadron (which didn't fit into any of the three categories) also applied a star for want of anything more suitable. Almost always an exception to a rule can be found!

Gauntlet IIs from 151 Squadron as they appeared in 1937. No. 151 Squadron had re-formed on 4 August 1936 with five Gauntlet IIs and by the time this photo was taken, at least two of its fighters had received metal three-blade Fairey Reed propellers in lieu of the older Watts wooden two-blade airscrew as seen on K5352 and K5353. Fitting the new component was a time-consuming task; one that entailed the installation of a new gun-interrupter unit to cater for a three-bladed propeller and thus prevent otherwise unsynchronized Vickers guns from firing straight into the blades.

Gauntlet II K7843 displays the distinctive red-bordered hollow arrowhead markings introduced by 46 Squadron when it re-formed in September 1936. Delivered to 46 Squadron in November 1936, K7843 was shipped to the Middle East a month or so after the unit re-equipped with Hurricanes in March 1939. Subsequently issued to 112 Squadron RAF, it later went to 3 Squadron RAAF with which it survived until SOC on 1 January 1944. While it is known that Gauntlets were used operationally across the region in 1940/41, they were more usefully employed in the ever-necessary pilot training role, so conserving the engine flying hours of the more valuable Gladiators.

A Gauntlet II from 74 Squadron seen while visiting Royal Air Force College Cranwell in 1937. The Squadron's distinctive tiger's head appears on the arrowhead located on the fin.

Unidentified 17 Squadron Gauntlet IIs seen at Kenley during the Munich crisis wearing a hastily-applied camouflage scheme that included black port-side and white starboard-side undersurfaces as a recognition feature. In this instance, however, the 'white' looks distinctly pale, so perhaps the original aluminium dope was retained on the starboard side as well as on the port ailerons. A further indicator of haste is the fact that this Gauntlet's serial number has been painted over and there is, as yet, no form of unit identification.

Seen at Sutton Bridge in February 1939 is this unidentified Gauntlet II 'RJ-Q' of 46 Squadron, 'RJ' being the unit's pre-war identification code (changing to 'PO' in September 1939). 'Q' was the aircraft's individual letter, the bottom portion of which is visible on the aft fuselage. Of academic interest, the undersurface colours are the reverse of those applied to the 17 Squadron example seen earlier. The rest of the airframe would have had a Dark Green and Dark Earth disruptive camouflage scheme applied, with the probability that the upper surfaces of the lower wings were painted Light Green/Light Earth, an effect known as the shadow compensating scheme.

A New Era Begins

While the Gloster Gladiator represented the final stage of British biplane fighter development, it also introduced modern features that were to become standard on RAF fighters for the first time, the most obvious of which, externally at least, was the inclusion of a fully-enclosed cockpit and a doubling of the standard armament of two fixed machine guns. The first seventy production machines were fitted with four Vickers .303in machine guns: two in the fuselage with 600 rpg, and two in remarkably flush fairings positioned beneath the lower wings with 400 rpg (the preceding development aircraft was fitted with drum-fed Lewis guns in somewhat larger under-wing fairings). Thereafter .303 Browning machine guns (developed from the American Browning .30 calibre machine gun) were installed with the same number of rounds per gun.

Unfortunately, ongoing and persistent problems existed with the Vickers machine gun inasmuch that although adapted for use in the air, it was based on the 500 rpm infantry weapon. The Air Ministry, well aware of the gun's importance in ground fighting, was equally aware that as the speed of aircraft increased, such targets could only remain in a fighter pilot's sights for a very short time. Consequently steps were taken to increase the gun's rate of fire to 850 rpm, which became the Vickers Mk III. Unfortunately, this had the effect of decreasing the reliability of both the gun and its associated components, with frequent stoppages caused by misfeeds (the ammunition feed proving slower than the gun firing mechanism), thus placing additional stresses on other components which often caused them to fail too. Hence the need to place breech blocks close by the pilot in the hope that he might be able to clear a stoppage in flight.

With the steady change from wood to metal construction, which included the prospect of armour being routinely added to military aircraft in the future, concerns arose as to whether or not a single pair of rifle-calibre guns might still be effective. Because trials with .5in rounds during the 1920s proved a disappointment, it was determined that the RAF should continue using rifle-calibre guns, with future fighters receiving multiple gun installations which, from the historical perspective and that of the RAF, usually means the eight-gun Hurricane and Spitfire with all guns located in the wings and firing outside of the propeller arc to obtain the highest possible concentration of fire. Occasionally history tends to forget the Gladiator when in fact it was the latter that became the RAF's first multi-gun fighter; i.e. a fighter equipped with more than two fixed machine guns as standard.

As for obtaining the Brownings, to cut a complex story short, following a decade of procrastination concerning .5in versus .303in, six Brownings were acquired and extensively tested until, in 1934, approval was given for sufficient '1930 Pattern' .303 Brownings to be obtained to equip two squadrons for extended trials. Of course, the choice of gun proved to be the correct one; it was reliable and, with a cyclic rate of 1,100 rpm, a fast-firing one. The fact that it was still being fitted to innumerable Spitfires, Seafires, Halifax and Lancaster bombers as late as 1945 remains a contentious issue more appropriately discussed elsewhere. However, it might be useful to recall that on the last day of the war Sub Lieutenant V. Lowden, an FAA Seafire III pilot, shot down a Japanese A6M5 'Zero' using his four .303s after having expended his 20mm ammunition in downing two other Zeros.

NB: As a footnote to the acquisition of the Browning machine gun, two parallel minor developments are probably worthy of comment as follows:

I) Vickers developed a prototype Mk IIIS machine gun, later called the Mk V. Despite having its cyclic rate reduced to approximately 720 rpm, the Mk V featured breech tolerances able to accept the ageing substandard .303in ammunition manufactured up to twenty years earlier. The result was a much more reliable weapon, albeit one that still couldn't match the Browning's reliability or rate of fire.

II) By the start of the Second World War the venerable hand-held Lewis gun had been replaced on most RAF front-line aircraft by the hand-held, drum-fed .303in Vickers Gas Operated/'Class K' gun [better known as the Vickers 'K', 'VGO' or simply 'K' gun] with a cyclic rate of 1,050 rpm and weighing just 19lb. When declared surplus to RAF requirements in 1943, the VGO had already become very popular with ground forces, the Long Range Desert Group particularly, because of its excellent reliability, high rate of fire and ease of maintenance.

K6145, the seventeenth production Gladiator I, was initially delivered to 74 Squadron on 9 March 1937, but a late change in policy dictated that 74 would replace its existing Demons with Gauntlets. Hence K6145 and four sisters were reassigned to 3 Squadron ten days later, the latter having recently become the RAF's second Gladiator unit, the honour of becoming the RAF's pioneer Gladiator unit having gone to 72 Squadron at the beginning of March. As seen here, K6145 wears 3 Squadron's solid green 'teardrop' fuselage band which was complemented by a tapering green bar on the upper wing. One item of interest to note is the under-wing gun barrel and muzzle; they appear to belong to a Vickers III or V machine gun as described earlier, rather than the slimmer Browning version. K6145 was serving with 263 Squadron by 10 October 1939, but was lost eleven days later when it flew into the River Severn and blew up.

Gladiator I L7612 from 33 Squadron is seen here at Ismailia, Egypt, in 1938 creating its own mini-sandstorm, much to the discomfort of the airman perched on the Gladiator's rear fuselage. Previously a light bomber squadron, the unit had been the first to fly the Hawker Hart, a fact commemorated by the unit's hart motif seen on L7612's fin. On 1 March 1938, however, 33 Squadron was reconstituted as a fighter unit, the only single-seat fighter unit outside the UK at that time. Eventually, as home-based fighter units re-equipped with monoplanes, it became possible to despatch small quantities of Gladiators (and Gauntlets) to the Middle East, East Africa and Aden to provide a core of fighter cover. Badly damaged in combat with Italian Fiat CR.42 biplane fighters over the Sudan in November 1940, L7612's pilot was forced to crash-land, writing the Gladiator off.

Gladiator I L7614, also belonging to 33 Squadron, being refuelled in Egypt in 1938. The flush-fitting under-wing gun fairing is shown to advantage in this view, although the gun is not installed. As with L7612, L7614 was shot down by CR.42s on the same day and destroyed. (*Tony O'Toole collection*)

Gladiator I K7985 from 73 Squadron in formation with another Gladiator from the same unit in 1937. The unit's colours on the fuselage and top wing consisted of a yellow central band with blue bands on either side. K7985 later served with 3 Squadron from March 1938, followed by 616, 605 and 263 Squadrons in turn. Stored from late October 1939, it was issued to 2 Anti-Aircraft Co-operation Unit (AACU) on 17 February 1942 with which it served until July that year, when it collided with another Gladiator and crashed.

Also from 73 Squadron, Gladiator I K7965 displays its upper wing markings to advantage during the halcyon days prior to Munich. This aircraft, like so many others, was transferred from one unit to another as required until it eventually arrived in the Middle East in June 1941. At some point thereafter K7965 joined the Western Desert Communication Flight, where it remained until finally coming to grief in February 1942 during a forced landing.

No. 80 Squadron Gladiator I K8011 seen in Egypt in 1938/39. This unit re-formed in March 1937 at Henlow before moving to Debden in June that year, where it remained until late April 1938 when the squadron was despatched to Egypt. The unit's motif on the fin, a bell, commemorated Major V. Bell, one of the unit's early commanders, the squadron motto being 'Strike true'. K8011 was SOC on 21 June 1941. (*Newark Air Museum*)

No. 87 Squadron Gladiator I K8027 seen at Debden in 1938. The markings on the fuselage consisted of a horizontal black bar (representing a tree) with a wavy green line (a serpent) entwined around it. In the First World War, 87 Squadron's identity marking had been a horizontally-presented letter 'S', but when the unit re-formed in March 1937, the 'S' was suitably modified to become a snake as seen on the fin. K8027 was SOC at Benina, Libya, when operating with 1563 Meteorological Flight following a landing accident there on 28 July 1943.

A sign of the times. This unidentified Gladiator was photographed during or shortly after the Munich crisis; an event that prompted the need to apply camouflage to many RAF aircraft, a process which, in this instance, completely obscured the serial number as well as removing any hint of the unit to which it belonged. In most cases, as seen here, the roundels on the upper wings and fuselage were made less visible by removing the white and reducing them to blue and red only, but in some instances the under-wing roundels were simply overpainted in black. Obviously armed, this Gladiator is fitted with Browning machine guns rather than Vickers. (*Tony O'Toole collection*)

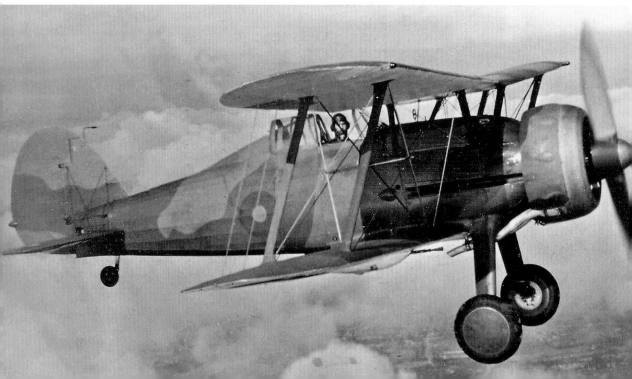

A Gladiator sits at Sutton Bridge on 6 February 1939. Although the serial number isn't known, the pre-war code letters 'OP' belonged to 3 Squadron which operated Gladiators until March 1938 when Hurricanes replaced them. However, due to a fatal crash at Kenley, 3 Squadron's home station, the airfield was deemed too small to operate Hurricanes and so they reverted to Gladiators in July 1938. Following a move to Biggin Hill, the unit began receiving Hurricanes once again from May 1939. Note that the Gladiator's black undersurfaces are the reverse of those applied to Gauntlet 'RJ-Q'.

After war was declared in 1939 the RAF sent two Gladiator units, 607 and 615 Squadrons, to France as part of the Air Component of the BEF. Here, Gladiator IIs of 615 Squadron are seen at St Inglevert, France, in April 1940, their unit codes having changed from 'RR' to 'KW' upon declaration of war. By this stage many Gladiators were finished in a four-colour shadow compensating upper camouflage scheme comprising Dark Earth and Dark Green with their lower wing upper surfaces and lower fuselage halves and fin finished in Light Green and Light Earth. No. 615's conversion to Hurricanes began, one flight at a time, in April 1940, although twelve or more Gladiators are believed to have still been on strength when the German offensive was launched in May. (*Newark Air Museum*)

A classic and rare view of a home-based Battle of Britain-era Gladiator II. Though hard to read, its code is 'HB-G' representing 239 Squadron, which re-formed as an army co-operation unit on 18 September 1940 using elements provided by 16 and 225 Squadrons. Primarily a Westland Lysander-equipped unit, 239 Squadron also acquired two refugee 615 Squadron Gladiators that initially went to 16 Squadron following their flight from France. The two Gladiators were N2304 and N2306 with the former, it is thought, becoming 'HB-G' seen here. The mark within the white tail stripe is believed to be the unit's motif of winged spurs. (*Tony O'Toole collection*)

The Monoplane Fighters

As might be expected in a book covering the years 1936 to 1939, the monoplane fighter features less prominently than its biplane equivalent, with just four types entering operational service during the period under review. One of these, the Boulton Paul Defiant, was a turret fighter which if nothing else epitomized the Air Ministry's fixation with the single-engined two-seat fighter, a legacy of the Bristol F.2B Fighter's success in the First World War. Presumably the Demon would in some way have emulated the F.2B had war with Germany erupted in 1937/38, although in retrospect one must wonder if procuring additional Hawker Fury single-seat fighters might have been a sounder policy; they were fast, already in production, and would have avoided the cost and effort of developing a new type of fighter and turret.

In fairness to the Demon, however, the pilot was at least equipped with a pair of fixed forward-firing guns which he would have used offensively while his gunner defended the aircraft's rear, as opposed to the pilot trying to solve the question of how best to position his aircraft so that the rear gun became the offensive weapon. F.2B crews had discovered the flaw in that tactic twenty years earlier. Sadly, for the new generation of turret fighters – the Defiant, Hotspur and Roc – the fateful decision was made to dispense with a fixed forward-firing armament. As a consequence the single-engined turret fighter, to put it kindly, came to represent a blind alley in British fighter design (other commentators have been far less kind; 'hopelessly inept' being but one observation).

More practical was the Bristol Blenheim IF, an adaptation of the famous Blenheim I twin-engined bomber, the first production examples of the latter having reached RAF squadrons in March 1937 and caused an immediate stir as once again a service bomber proved to be considerably faster than the RAF's latest fighter, the biplane Gladiator. Requiring little in the way of modification, approximately 200 Blenheim Is were converted to fighters with the first examples being cleared for operational use by October 1938. Blenheim IFs would be used for long-range patrols and night-fighting.

The remaining two fighters, the Hurricane and Spitfire, require no introduction except to say that their coverage here is probably less than the reader might have hoped for. The reason is that compared to other types, the quantities entering operational service were few initially; only from mid-1938 could it be said that Hurricane numbers were on the cusp of rising steadily. As for the Spitfire, while it is true that two squadrons did re-equip with this complex aircraft in 1938, in reality, propaganda aside, it wasn't until the end of 1939 that their numbers could be considered to have increased sufficiently to promote the belief that a reasonable degree of aerial security, over Britain at least, now existed.

Powered by a Rolls-Royce Merlin I engine, Defiant prototype K8310 first flew on 11 August 1937, albeit without its turret which was not then available. This image, taken in 1938, depicts both the turret and two of its four Browning .303in machine guns. K8310 was used for trials throughout its flying life until finally grounded in November 1941 when it became 2783M. (*Tony Buttler collection*)

Powered by a 1,030hp Merlin III, Defiant I L7012 is seen here prior to delivery. This aircraft went on to serve with 141, 255 and 256 Squadrons before becoming maintenance airframe 3227M in September 1941. No. 141 Squadron became the second operational Defiant unit after 264 Squadron which received them in December 1939, with 141 following from April 1940. Both units fought in the Battle of Britain. Although the type was credited initially with some impressive, albeit inflated, kill ratios against the Luftwaffe, the latter's fighters quickly got the measure of the Defiant, as demonstrated on 19 July 1940 when they decimated 141 Squadron. Even so, it had to soldier on. Against unescorted bombers the type had a chance despite its poor manoeuvrability and disappointing top speed of 302 mph (at 16,000ft), but against the Messerschmitt Bf 109E it was utterly outclassed, as much by faulty concept as design, the Defiant being 31 per cent heavier than the similarly-powered Hurricane. (*Tony O'Toole collection*)

Defiant I N1535 'PS-A' from 264 Squadron. The mount of Squadron Leader P. Hunter and gunner Pilot Officer F. King, N1535 was last seen chasing a Junkers Ju 88 bomber when it is believed to have been shot down by a Bf 109 off Dover on 24 August, 1940 killing both crewmen. (*Tony Buttler collection*)

Hawker Hotspur prototype K8309. First flown on 14 June 1938, the Hotspur, like the Defiant, was intended to replace the biplane Demon. Utilizing several components common to it and the Hawker Hurricane, the Hotspur was meant to compete with the Defiant, although it never did receive its intended four-gun turret, necessitating the installation of a wooden mock-up in lieu (the Hotspur also had provision for a fixed synchronized Vickers machine gun). Smaller than the Defiant and about 13 mph faster at c 16,000ft, the Hotspur never went into production as the need for Hurricanes was infinitely more important. Subsequently used for trials with its gun position faired over, K8309 was written off following a forced landing on 12 February 1942. (*Tony Buttler collection*)

Admittedly the Blackburn Roc was a Fleet Air Arm fighter with nothing whatsoever to do with the RAF. Based closely on the airframe of the two-seat Blackburn Skua naval reconnaissance fighter/dive-bomber, the Roc was yet another expression of the Air Ministry's fixation with the single-engined turret fighter. A navalized Defiant had been considered but the necessary wing folding requirements could not be easily met, and so Blackburn's proposal was accepted as a replacement for the navy's Hawker Osprey biplane fighter. Powered by an 890hp Bristol Perseus radial engine, the Roc was dismal, as too was its top speed of 223 mph at 10,000ft.

Displaying the squadron code 'YN' (changed to 'UF' in September 1939), these four unidentified Blenheim IF fighters belonged to 601 Squadron. Previously equipped with Gauntlets, Blenheim fighters were received in March 1939 and retained until February 1940 when they were replaced by Hurricane Is. Blenheim fighters, including the later IVF, were immediately distinguishable from the bomber versions by virtue of the tray fitted below the fuselage containing four Browning .303in machine guns (500 rpg) that supplemented the fixed gun in the port wing and the Vickers 'K' in the turret.

Blenheim IF K7159 'YX-N' joined 54 (Night Fighter) Operational Training Unit (OTU) on 10 December 1940, having previously served operationally with 61, 222 and 145 Squadrons. It remained with 54 OTU until it transferred to 51 OTU in August 1941. K7159 is of interest inasmuch as the airborne interception radar aerials on the port wing and nose suggest that K7159 was one of the twenty or so IFs fitted with the experimental AI Mk III radar that preceded the rather more useful AI Mk IV. This aircraft met its end on the night of 6 May 1943 when it crashed near Croxton Kerrial, Leicestershire.

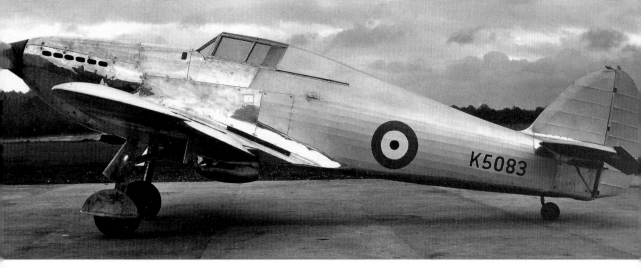

The solitary Hurricane prototype, K5083, as seen prior to its first flight on 6 November 1935. By comparison with production Hurricanes, the points of interest include the single canopy stiffener, tailplane struts and the short-lived D-shaped wheel covers which, hinged at 90 degrees to the undercarriage legs, suffered damage when taxiing over rough grass. To be armed originally with four Vickers machine guns (two in the nose plus two in the wings), the specification was modified to accept eight Brownings, although when this photo was taken weapons had yet to be fitted. Used for development purposes until production Hurricanes were available, K5083 became maintenance airframe 1211M on 14 January 1939. Returned to the manufacturer, this important aircraft survived into 1942 after which, presumably, it was scrapped as there doesn't seem to be any record of its ultimate fate. (*Tony Buttler collection*)

Lacking positive identification, this early Hurricane is probably L1583 from 111 Squadron, the latter becoming Fighter Command's first Hurricane squadron in December 1937. The initial production order covered 600 Mk Is commencing with L1547, the first 430 being completed with fabric-covered

wings, tailplane, fin, rudder and fuselage (aft of the cockpit). By April 1939, an all-metal wing with a stressed duralumin skin had been developed which was subsequently introduced on the production line, a development that enabled the Hurricane to dive at speeds nearly 80 mph greater than before. Though many surviving early Hurricanes would later exchange their original wings for the all-metal type, several were still operational during the Battle of Britain when they did at least exhibit one small advantage: cannon shells often passed right through them without exploding. (*Tony O'Toole collection*)

Hurricane Is L1550 and L1559 from 111 Squadron seen in 1938: the only visual evidence confirming that they belong to any unit at all is the diminutive 111 Squadron badge on each fin. This is a pre-Munich photo, confirmed by the fact that L1550 was written off following a crash on 18 July 1938, while L1559 survived until January 1939. The first Hurricanes lacked the type's distinctive ventral strake and rudder extension, features that would be incorporated on all Hurricanes from the 61st airframe onward to cure the fighter's poor spin recovery characteristics. No. 111 Squadron was allocated the unit code 'TM' in October 1938, changing to 'JU' in September 1939. (*Newark Air Museum*)

A now-familiar plan view of Hurricane I L1648, which went on to serve with 85 Squadron until it was damaged beyond repair at Debden on 6 October 1938 during the unit's transition from Gladiators to Hurricanes. Here the Watts two-blade, fixed-pitch wooden propeller fitted to all early Hurricanes is clearly seen. Inefficient at low airspeeds, aircraft fitted with it required a long ground run to get airborne. Subsequent trials with a De Havilland two-pitch (coarse/fine), three-blade metal Hamilton Standard propeller reduced the take-off run from 1,230ft to 750ft and Hurricanes began to receive the new propeller from April 1939. By the beginning of 1940, Rotol (a contraction of ROlls-Royce and BrisTOL) had developed a hydraulically operated, constant-speed propeller using Jablo compressed-wood blades, some of which were beginning to be fitted to Hurricanes around the time of the Battle of France. (*Tony Buttler collection*)

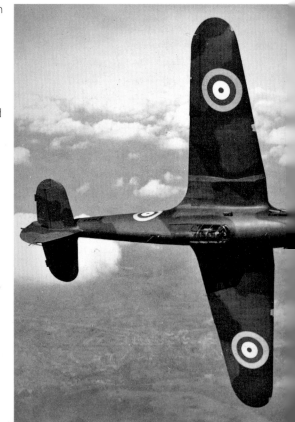

Hurricane I L1719 'AL-F' from 79 Squadron seen visiting a naval air station in 1939. The first Hurricanes were powered by a 1,030hp Rolls-Royce Merlin II or III engine driving the two-bladed Watts propeller seen here. As mentioned, Watts' propellers were replaced by metal two-pitch DH propellers, which in turn were surpassed by Rotol's constant-speed propeller unit (CSU) that transformed the Hurricane's performance and prompted DH to undertake a programme of modifying their older two-pitch propellers into a similar CSU. Thus, by the summer of 1940, most front-line Hurricanes were fitted with either a Rotol or De Havilland CSU.

The great improvement in propeller technology had as much to do with take-off performance and time-to-altitude as it did with maximum speed alone, but as for the question of 'How fast could a Hurricane I fly?', sources vary. Somewhere between 310 and 317 mph at 17,000ft was most often quoted. The Hurricane II series were faster by about 20 mph, but ultimately the speed-limiting factor was the Hurricane's thick wing and biplane-era method of construction. In short, while the Spitfire represented modern technology, the Hurricane represented the end of an older type, which didn't really matter in the summer of 1940 when ease of construction meant that the Hurricane was available in numbers at a critical moment in British history. (*Pat Chilton collection via Tony O'Toole*)

An undated image of Hurricane I L1791, complete with all-metal wings and three-bladed propeller. L1791 went on to serve with 46 Squadron and later 7 OTU. After losing power on 25 July 1940, the pilot managed to belly-land this aircraft which subsequently became maintenance airframe 2172M. Although the date of the photo is unknown, it is known that the Miles Magister I in the background (N541x) was delivered to the RAF between February and March 1939. (*Newark Air Museum*)

An unidentified Hurricane I seen operating from an airstrip somewhere in France during May or June 1940.

Also in France, Hurricane I 'VY-C' from 85 Squadron was photographed during May 1940 after the German onslaught had begun. Part of the unit code 'VY' is missing, but the hexagon on the Hurricane's fin confirms this as an 85 Squadron aircraft.

Flight Sergeant Geoffrey 'Sammy' Allard getting out of his 85 Squadron Hurricane I, probably during the Battle of Britain. This image shows to advantage the Rotol propeller and blades mentioned in previous captions with which most of this unit's Hurricanes had been fitted by the summer of 1940, much improving the Hurricane's take-off run and rate of climb. Later promoted to flight lieutenant, Allard had scored nineteen victories when he was killed in a flying accident on 13 March 1941. (*Newark Air Museum*)

The history of the Spitfire is well-known and hardly needs repeating here. Suffice to say that K5054, the prototype Spitfire, made its first flight on 5 March 1936, unpainted, with the undercarriage legs fixed down and without its undercarriage doors, hence this photo dates from a slightly later period. Powered by a prototype Merlin C of 990hp, the engine drove a Watts two-bladed, wooden fixed-pitch propeller. Following a number of early flights, the opportunity was taken to have undercarriage doors fitted to the legs and to replace its tailskid with a tailwheel. Originally unarmed, the wings were replaced in 1936 with a pair incorporating the now familiar set of eight .303in Browning machine guns.

Seen here with its original engine exhausts, on 19 September 1937, K5054 was flown with new ejector exhaust manifolds developed by Rolls-Royce which developed an additional 70lb of thrust, equivalent to about 70hp at 300 mph. K5054 came to the end of its flying life on 4 September 1939 while being tested at Farnborough. Following a misjudged landing, the aircraft bounced and then tipped onto its back, trapping the pilot who sustained serious neck injuries and died four days later. (*Tony Buttler collection*)

Mk I K9787 was the first production Spitfire from the first production order for 310 Spitfires, the order having been placed before K5054 had flown. K9787 first flew on 15 May 1938 and was delivered to the Aeroplane & Armament Experimental Establishment (A&AEE) at Boscombe Down in July. The first production Spitfires were powered by a 1,030hp Merlin II engine driving a Watts two-blade wooden propeller, but from the 78th airframe the latter was replaced by a De Havilland three-blade, two-pitch, metal propeller, and from the 175th airframe a Merlin III was fitted. Spitfire Is incorporating these modifications were able to achieve a maximum speed of 367 mph at 18,600ft and a service ceiling of 34,400ft. Meanwhile, other changes came about as a result of complaints from pilots, one of which led to a new 'curved-top' canopy hood being introduced to improve pilot headroom, hence modified hoods began to replace the original 'flat-topped' version (seen here) from early 1939. Later converted to the photo-reconnaissance role, K9787 was reported missing on 30 June 1941. (*Tony Buttler collection*)

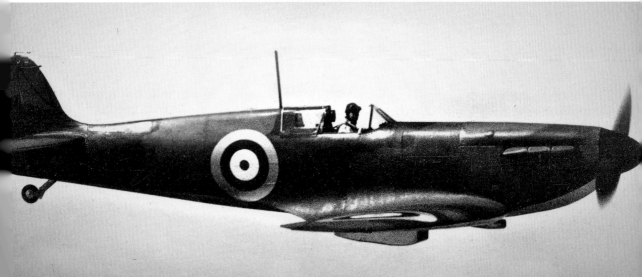

In August 1938, 19 Squadron began to transition from the Gauntlet to the Spitfire I and in so doing became the first RAF unit to receive the new fighter. Spitfire I K9851 (the 65th airframe) was delivered to 19 Squadron on 27 January 1939 and is seen here at Sutton Bridge about ten days later on 6 February. In this view it can be seen that the Spitfire's slender wing dictated that each of the four guns had to be widely spread to accommodate them, with two of the gun muzzles exposed in contrast to the Hurricane's much thicker wing that enabled its guns to be closely grouped and entirely enclosed within its confines.

A well-known photo of Spitfire I, K9906 'FZ-L', and others ('FZ-P' is K9956) from 65 Squadron seen in mid-1939, the unit having commenced its transition from Gladiators to Spitfires in March that year.

Spitfires from 616 Squadron as seen in late 1939, a few weeks after the unit had transitioned from the venerable Gauntlet. In order to facilitate the change from fixed undercarriage, open cockpit biplanes, a number of Fairey Battles were temporarily allocated to the unit. The fuselage code is 'QJ'.

Exuding a sense of urgency, ground crew prepare an unidentified Spitfire I for its next sortie. All that can be said with certainty here is that the part-serial number X4xxx (visible on the rear fuselage) confirms this to be one of a batch of 500 Spitfire Is delivered from July 1940, thus raising the possibility that this photo was taken during the Battle of Britain. (*Newark Air Museum*)

In June 1940, De Havilland began manufacturing a kit to convert their two-pitch propeller units into constant speed propellers. Although they were significantly heavier than the earlier types, (500lb compared to 350lb), it provided a substantial improvement in climb rate while also reducing take-off distances. Commencing on 24 June 1940, DH engineers began fitting all Spitfires with these units and by 16 August virtually every operational Spitfire (and Hurricane) had been modified. Such weight increases plus aerodynamic changes had led to later Spitfire Is having a lower maximum speed than the early production Mk Is, although this was more than offset by improvements in take-off distance and rate of climb brought about by the new CSUs. During the Battle of Britain period, Spitfire Is fitted with a CSU had a maximum speed of around 353 mph at 20,000ft. However, when supplies of 100 octane fuel from the USA began reaching Britain in early 1940, it meant that an emergency boost of +12lb per square inch was available for five minutes, boosting the Merlin III's power rating of 1,030hp to 1,310hp at 3,000rpm at 9,000ft and increasing maximum speed by 25 mph at sea level and 34 mph at 10,000ft, as well as improving climb performance.

Delivered in mid-1940, Spitfire I P9450 was photographed prior to joining 64 Squadron with which it operated until shot down by a Bf 109 over Kent on 5 December 1940. (*Tony Buttler collection*)

Vickers Type 279 Venom PVO-10 seen in 1936. Responding to Specification F.5/34 in 1934, Vickers produced the Venom, a fighter designed to overcome the performance advantages enjoyed by the fast day-bombers of the period. Using a 625hp Bristol Aquila radial engine (which hinged for easy access and servicing) and fitted with eight Browning machine guns, it was estimated that the Venom could achieve a maximum speed of 320 mph at 15,000ft. First flown on 17 June 1936 by 'Mutt' Summers, it proved very manoeuvrable and at 312 mph almost as fast as predicted. However, for a variety of reasons including a lack of engine development potential in comparison with the new Rolls-Royce PV12 (Merlin), the Venom proceeded no further and was scrapped in 1939, its demise hastened by the large orders previously placed for the Hurricane and Spitfire.

Glosters were awarded a contract to produce two prototype eight-gun F.5/34 fighters in response to Air Ministry Specification F5/34. Two prototypes, K5604 and K8089, were built, both powered by an 840hp Bristol Mercury IX radial engine with the first, K5604, flying in December 1937 and the second in March 1938, by which time the higher-performance Hurricane and Spitfire were already in production, consequently no further orders were forthcoming. The Gloster F.5/34 had a maximum speed of 316 mph at 16,000ft and a service ceiling of 32,000ft. (*Tony Buttler collection*)

P9594, the Martin-Baker Aircraft Company's MB.2 interceptor, was another contender for an eight-gun fighter as per Specification F5/34. Fitted with a 1,000hp Napier Dagger III engine driving a wooden two-blade propeller, the MB.2 achieved 305 mph at just under 10,000ft and featured a fixed 'trousered' undercarriage. No production orders ensued. (*Tony Buttler collection*)

The Miles Master I was an advanced trainer powered by a 715hp Rolls-Royce Kestrel XXX engine. Of the several hundred Master Is procured by the RAF, twenty-four (or twenty-six) were built in such a way that they could be quickly transformed into the Miles M.24 Emergency Fighter by removing the rear seat and a section of cockpit glazing and installing three .303in Browning machine guns in each wing. The top speed of a Master I was 226 mph at 15,000ft, and presumably the same would have applied to the M.24 too; fortunately the question of how effective it might have been against the Luftwaffe remains a matter of conjecture as they were never called into action! While serving with 9 FTS, N7412, which was one of the 'six-gun' fighters, inexplicably dived into the ground on 23 July 1941. (*Tony O'Toole collection*)

Chapter Two

The Bombers

Prior to the commencement of hostilities, Bomber Command had introduced the Armstrong Whitworth Whitley and Vickers Wellington to its arsenal, the former being described as a long-range heavy night-bomber and the latter as a medium/heavy by the standards of the day, the pair being supplemented by Handley Page's relatively fast and agile Hampden medium-bomber. Confidence was high among the bomber crews, particularly those operating aircraft fitted with power-operated turrets. There seemed to be no doubt in the minds of many that in daylight bombing operations the power-operated turret was the master of any fighter pilot foolish enough to wander within range of well-defended bombers once war commenced. Time would tell a different tale!

By mid-1939 the three modern designs had replaced all remaining front-line biplane 'heavies' in addition to the monoplane Fairey Hendon night-bomber and single-engined Vickers Wellesley 'interim' medium/light bomber, with the Command's remaining Handley Page Harrows relegated to their alternative (but vital) role as transports.

Broadly similar in concept to the Harrow, the delayed Bristol Bombay bomber-transporter was only just entering operational service when the war commenced with most being consigned to the Middle East where they were frequently called upon to operate as bombers alongside Blenheims and recently-displaced Wellesleys. Bomber Command's light bomber category was represented by the Blenheim, particularly the Mk IV, and single-engined Fairey Battles.

The Westland Wapiti is best remembered for its exploits over Iraq and the North-West Frontier where it served as a robust two-seat bombing and general-purpose (GP) aircraft able to carry a bomb load of about 580lb. Less well remembered is the fact that Wapitis also served at home with 501 Special Reserve Squadron and Auxiliary Air Force (AAF) day-bomber squadrons from 1929 until Harts began replacing them in 1933. However, two AAF units retained Wapitis into January 1937, hence the type qualifying for inclusion in this section. Wapiti IIA, J9601, from 602 Squadron is seen here prior to the unit re-equipping with Harts from February 1934.

An unidentified Westland Wapiti IIA from 605 Squadron. The unit received its first Hawker Harts in February 1934 and then used both types until November that year when the last Wapitis were disposed of. (*Newark Air Museum*)

Both 607 and 608 Squadrons retained the Wapiti IIA until January 1937, after which the type was removed from the RAF's home-based order of battle. Thereafter, many were transferred to secondary duties or Commonwealth countries where some continued to serve well into 1943. K2242 was one of sixteen Wapiti VI dual-control trainers built in 1931 for allocation on an individual basis to the day-bomber Wapiti units. Having re-equipped with Demons, both 607 and 608 Squadrons became fighter rather than bomber units, albeit 608 Squadron underwent a further role change on 20 March 1939 when it was transferred to Coastal Command and re-equipped with Avro Ansons. (*Newark Air Museum*)

The Westland Wallace, like the Wapiti, was a general-purpose machine; a type much desired by Britain's cash-strapped governments of the 1930s because they could undertake a variety of tasks with minimal alteration to the basic design. Initially known as the Wapiti VII, the name was soon changed to Wallace because of the many differences between them. All the more ironic then that despite it being a GP machine, both the Wallace I and II served exclusively as home-based day-bombers with 501, 502, 503 and 504 Special Reserve Squadrons from 1933 (501), 1934 (504) and 1935 (502 and 503) until mid-1937. Thereafter the surviving airframes served for many years in valuable if perhaps mundane non-operational roles.

K3566, seen here, served with 501 Squadron from 18 March 1933 until 11 February 1937. Subsequently sent to various training units, its last was the Ground Defence Gunners School (GDGS) in the Isle of Man which used Wallaces and Gauntlets to train gunners for airfield defence. K3566 was SOC on 1 September 1941.

The Fairey Gordon (originally the Fairey IIIF Mk V) was issued to home-based day-bomber squadrons and to GP units in the Middle East. When the Second World War commenced, twenty-seven remained in the Middle East with perhaps ten more flyable in the UK, all by then relegated to target tug and flying training duties. However, when the Iraqi army attacked the RAF base at Habbaniya in May 1941, Gordons and other elderly 4 FTS aircraft, fitted with guns and bomb racks, were returned briefly to operational service. The last were grounded in 1942 and scrapped. This particular example, Gordon I K2635, was allocated to Middle East-based 14 Squadron which used the type until replaced by Vickers Wellesleys from March 1938. (*Newark Air Museum*)

An unidentified Fairey Gordon from 35 Squadron which operated the type until replaced by Wellesleys in July 1937. The pilot's Vickers machine gun (visible below the characters DTD224) was supplemented by a Lewis machine gun in the observer's cockpit; still very much a First World War armament, as indeed it was on the Wapiti, Wallace, Hart, Hind and many other aircraft of the period.

Hawker Hind K5401 belonged to 44 Squadron when it was photographed in 1937, the unit being one of forty or more squadrons to which the Hind was ultimately issued. A development of the Hart, the latter had been largely replaced in Bomber Command by mid-1936. By late 1937, 340 Hinds were serving with Bomber Command with 115 more allocated to AAF squadrons, although with the arrival of the Fairey Battle and Bristol Blenheim in increasing numbers, several were subsequently converted to dual-control trainers. The last operational unit to retain the Hind was probably 613 Squadron, an army co-operation unit formed in March 1939 which, nominally at least, retained them until April 1940, thereafter leaving 613 Squadron to soldier on with the Hawker Hector. K5401 was written off following a crash in August 1940.

An 83 Squadron Hind being readied for its next flight in 1937 or 1938. Clearly visible, the observer's Lewis gun and the trough for the pilot's Vickers gun are as indicative of the First World War as are the four 112lb HE RL (Royal Laboratory) bombs of much the same vintage. Assuming they are not inert, then each bomb would be filled with either 60lb or 35lb of high explosive depending on the weight of casing employed. Hinds carried a maximum bomb load of 510lb.

To include or not? Put simply, its purpose is to help illustrate the extent to which British bomber design was to advance in a relatively short period of time. As fascinating as the twin-engined biplane bomber was, their pedestrian and ponderous characteristics could not be denied. Despite this, some remained operational almost to the eve of Munich itself, and beyond for the Handley Page Heyford. For the record, this is a Handley Page H.P.24 Hyderabad, a type that served from 1925 until retired by 503 Squadron in January 1934. The Hyderabad was the RAF's last heavy bomber to be constructed of wood. It had a wingspan of 75ft and a maximum speed of 109 mph.

Equally impressive was the Vickers Virginia X night-bomber, one of which from 500 Squadron is seen here in 1935. This unit would relinquish its Virginias in 1936, as indeed would 7 and 9 Squadrons, while 214 and 215 Squadrons retained theirs until 1937, with 58 Squadron retaining its Virginias until January 1938. It is perhaps surprising therefore to learn that when 51 and 75 Squadrons re-formed in 1937, both received Virginias (plus a few Avro Ansons). The last front-line Virginia unit, 51 Squadron, surrendered them in February 1938, but even then some of the breed continued to fly on non-operational duties until the last one expired in September 1941 at Henlow. The Virginia X had a wingspan of 87ft 8in and a maximum speed of 108 mph.

A Virginia X which, aside from its individual identity letter 'V', remains anonymous, as indeed does the squadron to which it belonged. (*Newark Air Museum*)

The Handley Page Heyford was the RAF's last heavy multi-engined biplane night-bomber. Its configuration was absolutely distinctive; one that couldn't be confused with any other aircraft of the day. Shown here is Handley Page H.P.38 J9130, the prototype Heyford which flew for the first time on 12 June 1930. Used primarily for trials purposes, this aircraft crashed into a sea wall near North Coates, Lincolnshire on 8 July 1932. (*Newark Air Museum*)

Heyford I K3489 was the first of 124 production Heyfords to be built. First flown on 21 June 1933, K3489 is seen here on 25 November 1933. Procured to replace the Virginia, Heyfords became the standard RAF night-bomber of the mid-1930s, the type's operational debut commencing with 99 Squadron in November 1933. Issued to several bomber squadrons, seven were still equipped with Heyfords in May 1939 of which two, 166 and 149 Squadrons, retained Heyford IIIs and Is until July and August 1939 respectively. K3489 was SOC on 23 January 1939, the result of a heavy landing four months earlier. (*Newark Air Museum*)

Heyford I K3489 shown at rest.

Heyford I K3500 'R' was delivered to 99 Squadron on 9 March 1934 and remained until May 1937 when it was damaged following a forced landing and subsequently SOC. This image shows all three gun positions, including the retractable ventral 'dustbin' turret, each with a single Lewis gun. Heyfords carried a normal bomb load of 2,660lb enclosed in cells located in the lower wing centre section, their proximity to the ground enabling the re-arming process to be completed more rapidly than with other types (additional bombs could also be carried on external Light Series bomb racks). All Heyfords had a wingspan of 75ft while maximum speed varied according to the mark and engines fitted (Mk I 138 mph; Mk IA 142 mph; Mk II and III 154 mph). (*Newark Air Museum*)

Heyford II (or IIA?) K4033 'F' with four-bladed propellers belonging to 10 Squadron in 1935/36.

The part-visible serial number K6(???) seen on the lower wing identifies 'S' as a Heyford III, all fifty of which were delivered between January and July 1936.

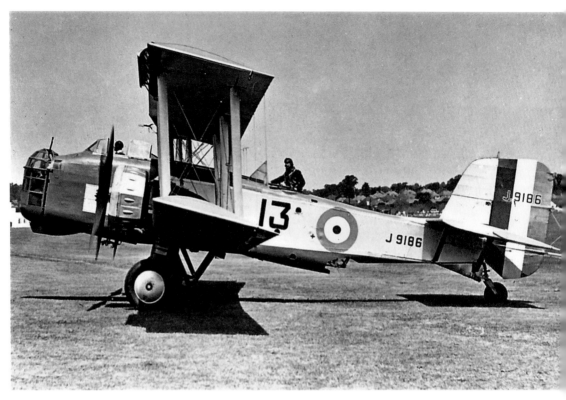

Perhaps more than any other RAF inter-war biplane bomber, the Boulton Paul Overstrand was considerably more innovative than first impressions might convey. The Overstrand featured an enclosed cockpit, provision for an automatic pilot, a hot air supply for each crew member and a fully enclosed power-operated turret in the nose, the first of its kind to be fitted on any RAF aircraft. Essentially, the turret was a vertical cylinder with domed ends mounting a single Lewis gun, the barrel of which projected through a vertical slot that ran the whole length of the turret with an 'automatic fastener' to prevent a blast of cold air from passing through the slot into the heated turret itself. The turret could rotate through 360 degrees and, if elevated sufficiently, the gun could be brought to bear aft over the upper wing. Despite being a five-seat medium day-bomber, Overstrands (like their forebear the Sidestrand) often operated with a crew of just three, hence only one rear gunner. The reasoning was that because they were intended to operate in formation, fixed individual positions within that formation would be confirmed prior to take-off, thereby supplying the answer as to which of the two gun positions would be armed.

Twenty-four production Overstrands were constructed with a handful of others converted from Sidestrands, one of which, J9186 (shown here), became the prototype Sidestrand V until March 1934 when the name was changed to Overstrand. This image shows to advantage all three Lewis gun positions and the ample slipstream protection provided for the dorsal gun position. The number '13' was allocated for its appearance at the Hendon Display on 30 June 1934. (*Tony O'Toole collection*)

Completed as a Sidestrand III, J9770 was converted to an Overstrand after a Fairey IIIF taxied into it on 1 July 1932. In the event, J9770 never joined an RAF unit, being allocated instead for use in test and handling trials, some associated with in-flight refuelling. It is believed that J9770 made its last flight in the hands of the Royal Aircraft Establishment (RAE) on 9 September 1938. Given the quantity procured, only 101 Squadron was ever fully equipped with the Overstrand, which flew them from January 1935 until August 1938, when they were finally replaced by Blenheim Is. Subsequently a few Overstrands lingered on as gunnery trainers at Dumfries until 1940/41 (NB: when 144 Squadron re-formed in January 1937, they did so using Ansons plus four Overstrands on temporary loan). (*Newark Air Museum*)

The Monoplane Bombers

In an era of biplane bombers, the Fairey Hendon long-range night-bomber created a modern image when it entered service with 38 Squadron in November 1936, the type being the first all-metal low-wing cantilever monoplane bomber to enter RAF service, although in truth it was already outdated and offered little improvement over the Heyford in operational terms. Production ran to a mere fourteen airframes, all of which went to 38 Squadron at Marham which retained them until the eleven survivors were sent to maintenance units (MU) in January 1939. Most became ground instructional airframes with five seeing out their days within the Electrical & Wireless Schools. This photograph shows Hendon prototype K1695 in company with a Heyford, possibly at A&AEE Boscombe Down in May 1934 when both were involved in comparative trials. (*Newark Air Museum*)

The prototype Hendon K1695 was easily distinguished from production airframes as it lacked a cockpit canopy. In order to lend scale to this image, the Hendon's wingspan at 101ft 9in was just 3in less than an Avro Lancaster! K1695 was struck off charge in January 1939, its last duties being with Flight Refuelling Limited.

Hendon K5085 illustrates the external changes that were incorporated on production airframes compared to K1695, namely a cupola for the front gunner, enclosed cockpit canopy, a modified 'chin' with bomb-aiming window, plus three-bladed propellers. Production airframes were designated Hendon II and were defensively armed with a single Lewis gun in each of the three positions seen in this image. The Mk II carried a maximum bomb load of 1,660lb and could achieve 155 mph at 15,000ft, almost exactly the same as the Overstrand, although the latter's range of 540 miles was about 800 miles less than the Hendon. (*Newark Air Museum*)

Hendon II K5087 was adapted to become a 'DC' or dual-control trainer, the cockpit extension being quite evident in this view. One other Hendon, K5094, was similarly adapted. (*Tony Buttler collection*)

The end of Hendon II K5087. (*Tony Buttler collection*)

Handley Page Harrow interim heavy bomber and transport. On 10 October 1936, K6933, shown here, became the first of 100 production Harrow Mks I and II to be constructed, with this airframe doubling as the prototype. When first flown its gun positions were all faired over but by the time this photo was taken in early 1937, interim fixed glazing had been fitted prior to the later installation of power-operated turrets in the nose and tail positions with a single Lewis gun in the nose and twin Lewis machine guns in the tail position. A manually-operated dorsal cupola with a fourth gun supplemented the armament. The Harrow was the first production bomber for the RAF to receive the soon-to-be familiar Temperate Land Scheme of Dark Green and Dark Earth which was applied in the equally familiar disruptive camouflage pattern seen here.

K6933 served with 214 Squadron from early 1937 prior to participating in in-flight refuelling trials in 1938. Placed on the civil register in April 1939, the Harrow was then shipped to Newfoundland for flight refuelling trials with C-class flying boats before being handed to the Royal Canadian Air Force in October 1940 as number 794. (*Carl Vincent via Tony O'Toole*)

An unidentified Harrow displays the new disruptive camouflage scheme of Dark Green and Dark Earth, albeit with just a single roundel on the wing. Less obviously, a power-operated gun turret has been fitted to the nose in which only the guns, located at the base of the turret, rotated, with the rest of the structure remaining fixed. Seldom photographed from above, the dorsal cupola is also evident in this view. During the course of the type's service as an operational bomber, Lewis guns were subsequently replaced by the Vickers 'K' and, later still reportedly, by Brownings in some instances.

Harrow II K6988 'J' of 214 Squadron seen in 1938, this unit having become the first to receive Harrows in January 1937. Always intended as a transport, such was the pressing need for modern heavy bombers they were instead issued to Bomber Command (37, 75, 115, 214 and 215 Squadrons) in 1937, the Command retaining them until sufficient Wellingtons were on hand to replace them in mid-1939. Harrows could accommodate 3,000lb of bombs, had a maximum speed of 200 mph and a range of 1,250 miles. Following their service as bombers, the type reverted to their intended role in which they provided sterling service. (*Tony Buttler collection*)

When the Bristol Type 142 fast transport (the famed 'Britain First') first flew on 12 April 1935, it was found to be capable of speeds in excess of 300 mph in level flight at a time when the 230 mph Gloster Gauntlet had barely begun to enter RAF service. The Bristol Type 142 was also about 50 mph faster than the forthcoming Gloster Gladiator. The Air Ministry naturally displayed a keen interest in the Type 142 from which the very similar Bristol Type 142M bomber, soon to become the Blenheim I, would evolve. An initial order for 150 examples of the Type 142M was placed in September 1935, the first of which, K7033 (shown here), flew for the first time on 25 June 1936 and was delivered to the RAE on 19 April 1937. K7033 was ultimately SOC in December 1943 as scrap. (*Tony Buttler collection*)

Seen at Great West Road Aerodrome (today's Heathrow Airport) in May 1938, Blenheim I K7170 'V' belonged to 61 Squadron who chose to display individual aircraft codes on their engine cowlings rather than the fuselage. Having re-formed in March 1937, 61 Squadron received its first Blenheim in January 1938, with K7170 being delivered a month later. No. 114 Squadron had been the first unit to receive the Blenheim in March 1937, with four more squadrons following suit that year and twelve more in 1938, one of which, 30 Squadron, was based in the Middle East. (The newly-forming Blenheim IF fighter units are not included in these figures.)

Blenheim I bombers on the assembly line at Filton, Bristol in 1938. Points of interest include the raised dorsal turret which, when not in use, could be partially lowered to reduce drag, and the fabric-covered port in the leading edge of the left wing, immediately above the screw jacks, which housed the Blenheim's other gun. Of the two identifiable airframes, L1164 was lost on the first day of the war when it stalled and crashed during a single-engine approach near Hendon, while L1170 survived until SOC on 17 August 1943.

Blenheim I L1295. This image helps to illustrate the sleek and modern lines of an aircraft which in 1936 was well ahead of its time. Unfortunately, because the type's operational record has been extensively commented upon, both during the war and ever since, the Blenheim is now remembered not only for the many acts of valour displayed by its crews, but also because of the appalling operational losses it suffered in terms of air crew and aircraft. Thus history largely manages to overlook the Blenheim's technical superiority and pre-war relevance.

Equally, ever pragmatic, history also reveals the hard-nosed truth that as early as May 1940, the Blenheim had already been overtaken by accelerating technologies and by 1941 was in dire need of urgent replacement. Advances in modern fighter development soon proved lethal to the Blenheim, as did the often overlooked lethality of German anti-aircraft weapons (flak) in the 20 to 40mm category, the nemesis of many low-flying tactical bombers. (*Tony Buttler collection*)

No. 45 Squadron's first Blenheim loss occurred on 10 July 1939 at Amman, Jordan, when L8500 swung on landing and was damaged beyond repair. Depending on how one interprets the handwritten note on the rear of the photo, it is possible to conclude that L8500, the unit's very first Blenheim, met its premature end at the conclusion of its delivery flight, which might explain the absence of both squadron code and individual identifying letter.

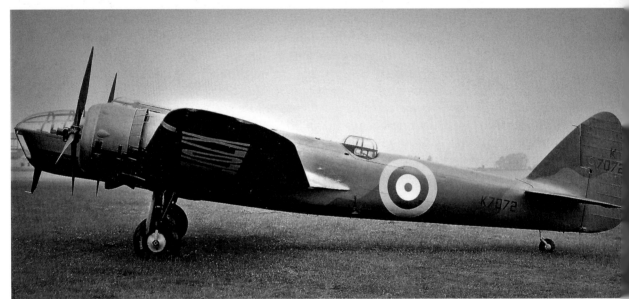

Two views of Blenheim K7072 which, ordered as a Mk I, was set aside for long-nose trials resulting from complaints voiced by bomber crews virtually from the outset concerning the cramped navigator's position in the nose. Following a series of trials a glazed asymmetric nose extension was found to be acceptable, incorporating as it did a scalloped section in front of the pilot as shown here, and sufficient space for the navigator to be seated in the starboard side of the nose with a map table located beneath the port-side glazing.

Designated the Blenheim IV (the Mk II and III were one-off development stages, neither of which went into production), the opportunity was also taken to increase the new mark's fuel capacity by incorporating a 94-gallon tank in each outer wing, bringing its total capacity up to 468 gallons. This in turn meant more weight requiring more powerful engines, although the best that could be achieved was to substitute the Blenheim I's 840hp Bristol Mercury VIII engines with the 920hp Mercury XV.

Although the first Bomber Command squadrons to receive the new Mark were 82 and 90 Squadrons in March 1939, the first Mk IVs had in fact been delivered to 53 Squadron, an army co-operation unit, two months earlier in January. Despite this, by September 1939 the majority of Bomber Command's Blenheim units were operational on the Blenheim IV. (*Both images: Carl Vincent via Tony O'Toole*)

An unidentified production Blenheim IV seen c April 1940. The prominent under-wing 'horns' are dump tubes fitted to enable fuel in the outer tanks to be jettisoned, thus shedding weight quickly should the need to make an otherwise fully-loaded landing occur. Warlike changes include drag-inducing Light Series bomb racks beneath the rear fuselage for the carriage of 40lb and 25lb bombs or flares to supplement the usual internal bomb load of four 250lb bombs. Defensively, twin Browning .303 machine guns have replaced the single Vickers 'K' previously mounted in the turret. Although this is a wartime image, the code 'XJ' signifies 13 OTU. (*Tony Buttler collection*)

Able to carry approximately 5,500lb of ordnance, depending upon mark, Armstrong Whitworth's Whitley was the RAF's heavy bomber during the immediate pre-war years and remained so into 1941. Seen here in an overall silver finish is the prototype Whitley, K4586, which made its first flight on 17 March 1936 powered by two 795hp Armstrong Whitworth Tiger IX radial engines.

In August 1935, an order for eighty Whitleys was placed for delivery to the RAF before the prototype had even flown, such was the urgency of the rearmament programmes. Of the eighty airframes ordered, thirty-four were Whitley Is, all of which were delivered between March and October 1937, with K7183, seen here, being the first production example. The remaining forty-six airframes were Mk IIs powered by 845hp Tiger VIIIs rather than the Tiger IX fitted to the Mk I. They in turn were followed by eighty Mk IIIs and forty Mk IVs. Dispatched to the A&AEE in March 1937 for performance testing, K7183 was photographed there during that month with the first production Hawker Hector, K8090, in the background. (*Tony Buttler collection*)

Whitley I K7191 was the subject of a set of publicity images used to herald the recent inclusion of a modern 'heavy' to Bomber Command's order of battle. Despite the many shortcomings of early Whitleys, to the public the type must have been seen as a great leap forward when compared to the recently-introduced Hendon and Harrow, not to mention the remaining Virginia and Heyford biplane bombers. K7191 was delivered to 10 Squadron on 24 May 1937, two months after it became the first Whitley unit. Although early Mk Is lacked the dihedral applied to the outer wing sections of all subsequent models, it was applied on the production line to a few of the later Mk Is and retrospectively to surviving 'straight-wing' examples. Rounded tail fins remained a feature until they were replaced by the 'squared-off' version introduced by the Mk V. In terms of defence the Mk I and II were fitted with manually-operated turrets in nose and tail with a single gun in each. The Mk III introduced a power-operated nose turret (Vickers 'K') as well as a retractable ventral 'dustbin' turret with two Browning machine guns which, when lowered, proved to be little more than a half-ton, drag-inducing hindrance. It was excluded from later marks. (*Tony Buttler collection*)

Whitley I K7184 with 4° dihedral applied retrospectively. Having joined 166 Squadron in June 1939, K7184 received the code 'AS-A' and remained with the unit until March 1940; thereafter it went to various training establishments before ending its days at the PEE (Proof and Experimental Establishment) at Shoeburyness where it arrived on 14 December 1942.

An unidentified Whitley III with scarcely visible under-wing serial numbers which appear to commence with K89xx and minus under-wing roundels. The bombardier's glazed 'chin' extension was fitted retrospectively.

Bomber Command's first Whitleys, the Marks I, II and III, were all fitted with Tiger radial engines, whereas later marks, the IV and V (plus Coastal Command's Mk VII from late 1941), received Merlins. Mark I K7208 was retained by the manufacturer to become a Merlin-powered Whitley IV prototype, this photograph having been taken towards the end of 1938 while allocated to Rolls-Royce. The lack of a turret – front, rear or both – was not unusual as their production frequently lagged behind airframe production although, given its status, it is likely that K7208 never did receive them. The Whitley IV also introduced the innovative four-gun power-operated (rear) turret to Bomber Command which, by 1939 standards, was able to supply withering firepower; a match for any aircraft attacking from the rear if it strayed within range. Only ever used for trials and evaluation, K7208 crash-landed in June 1941 and became a ground instruction airframe.

A close-up of a Merlin II engine installation.

Whitley IV K9025, one of thirty-three Mk IVs to be delivered, was powered by two 1,030hp Merlin IV engines as opposed to the Tiger engines of preceding marks. While the Merlin's additional power improved performance, sources vary considerably regarding the extent, although it would seem that the Mk IV, at normal operating weight, could achieve a cruising speed of about 195 mph at 15,000ft compared to approximately 164 mph for the Mk III at the same altitude. Such detail rather misses the point, however, given that Tiger-engined Whitleys were notoriously unable to maintain height on one engine, with several being lost due to engine failure on night-time training flights.

The Mk IV, in retaining the type's original fin and introducing the four-gun tail turret, also introduced a glazed 'chin' extension for the bombardier that replaced a hinged panel on earlier marks, some of which were fitted with a new 'chin' retrospectively. K9025 was delivered to 10 Squadron on 31 May 1939 and served operationally until it was transferred to 10 OTU in May 1940. It met its end on 18 April 1942 when it hit a hangar at Kinloss following an engine failure on take-off.

Originally forty Whitley IVs were ordered, of which seven, including K9055, were modified to accept the Merlin X powerplant, the first Merlin to be fitted with a two-speed supercharger for operational use (1,145hp c 5,200ft/1,010hp c 17,600ft). Sources vary regarding the precise nomenclature of these seven airframes: some list them as Mk IVs, while others refer to them as the Mk IVa. Suffice to say that the definitive Whitley, the Mk V, employed the same Merlin X as did the IVa.

K9055 was delivered to 78 Squadron on 11 August 1939, with which it remained until transferred to 19 OTU in June 1940. Flown to 44 Maintenance Unit (MU) in February 1943, it was SOC six months later.

N1352 was the eighth Whitley V built from an eventual total of 1,466 and was photographed during the last days of peace in August 1939. The Mk V introduced a 'square-cut' fin, a 15in fuselage extension to improve the rear turret's field of fire and de-icing boots in the wing leading edges. As production gathered pace it became the mark upon which Bomber Command leaned heavily to conduct leaflet-drops and night bombing raids against the Axis forces during the early years of the war. In fact they would continue to employ the Whitley V against targets in occupied Europe until the night of 29 April 1942 when it was finally withdrawn from the Command's order of battle. However, lest it be thought that in September 1939 Bomber Command was awash with Whitleys, it is sobering to reflect that at that time the RAF possessed just 195, of which 45 were Merlin-powered examples including six Mk Vs. The remainder were Tiger-powered examples, some of which were used to drop leaflets over Germany. While 195 might appear to be a reasonable number, that figure reduces significantly if serviceability and operational training are considered, hence the number of Whitleys available for operational use would have been noticeably less.

N1352 ditched in the North Sea on 19 April 1940 following an attack on Trondheim, Norway.

From the same production batch as N1352, 102 Squadron's Whitley V, N1421 'DY-C', is seen here in early 1940 at Driffield, its home base. This aircraft was shot down by flak on 30 April 1940. (*Tony Buttler collection*)

Whitley V, N1386 'DY-P', also from 102 Squadron, is seen here being happily loaded with propaganda leaflets prior to being dropped on unsuspecting Germans! Having served with 102 Squadron, N1386 went on to serve with 19 and 10 OTU until it was SOC in June 1945. Reportedly, it was a Whitley from this squadron that is believed to have been the first RAF aircraft to deliberately drop bombs on German soil (as opposed to ships in harbour mouths or estuarial waters) on the night of 19/20 March 1940 in retaliation for an attack on Scapa Flow three days earlier in which a civilian was killed. (*Tony Buttler collection*)

One presumes that this also is a staged photo given that a Whitley's five-man crew normally entered via the larger fuselage door aft of the main spar rather than the emergency exit seen here, but I could be wrong!

In September 1935, Vickers received orders from the Air Ministry for a total of ninety-six monoplane long-range day/night bombers. Production airframes were preceded by the single prototype K7556 which used geodetic construction to combine light weight with torsional stiffness. Powered by a single 670hp Bristol Pegasus engine and with a wing span of 74ft 7in, K7556 first flew on 15 June 1935. Used extensively in development, test and performance duties, it was eventually grounded in March 1940.

Subsequently named Wellesley, the first production example, K7713, made its first flight on 30 January 1937, with K7717, the subject of this photo, following suit shortly afterwards. Delivered to 7 Squadron on 9 April 1937, K7717 was almost immediately reallocated to 76 Squadron followed by 148 Squadron in August. Wearing the latter's unit markings on its fuselage, by the time this image was taken it had already been seconded to Vickers-Armstrong for long-range trials associated with the Pegasus XXII engine shown here. Damaged beyond repair following a crash, K7717 was SOC on 15 July 1938. (*Tony Buttler collection*)

A total of 176 Wellesleys were produced, five of which were allocated to the Long Range Development Unit established at Upper Heyford in early 1938. Distinguishable from standard Wellesleys by their long-chord engine cowlings (as seen on test-bed K7717), three of them – L2638, L2639 and L2680 – were chosen to attempt a non-stop distance record. Thus, on 5 November 1938, the trio departed Ismailia, Egypt and headed for Darwin, Australia, 7,162 miles away. Two completed the journey in a little over forty-eight hours to successfully establish a new world record while the third, L2639, diverted to Timor due to higher than expected fuel consumption. (For the record, the other two LRDU Wellesleys were L2637 and L2681, both of which later served in the Middle East.)

L2638 suffered a forced landing near Windsor, New South Wales, in late November 1938. Seen here with its damaged propeller stowed beneath the fuselage, L2638 was subsequently shipped back to Britain whilst L2680 was shipped to Egypt.

According to the handwritten note on the rear of the photo, this Wellesley is L2639. Sadly, the airmen's names were not recorded but one wonders if the officer on the right with two rings on his sleeve might be Flight Lieutenant H.A.V. Hogan who piloted this aircraft on 5 November 1938. After suffering a forced landing in Australia five weeks later, L2639 later became an instructional airframe at an engineering facility near Melbourne and so never returned to the UK. At least one other Wellesley, K7734, was also allocated to the LRDU, however, both it and its crew went missing on 24 February 1938 during a trial long-distance flight around Britain. On that day a radio message was received from the aircraft whilst in the vicinity of Orkney, following which all communication ceased. On 22 March, a tail wheel and other minor bits of wreckage which might have come from K7734 were found floating in the sea approximately 20 miles north of Stavanger, Norway.

Typical RAF Wellesleys were powered by a 925hp Pegasus XX radial engine that enabled the bomber to achieve a cruising speed of 180 mph at 15,000ft. The type could lift a maximum bomb load of 2,000lb using under-wing panniers as the Wellesley's geodetic construction made it difficult to fit an internal bomb bay. For defence they were equipped with a fixed Browning .303 machine gun in the starboard wing, supplemented by a Vickers 'K' for the gunner/bomb-aimer in a second cockpit widely separated from the pilot. Wellesleys usually operated with a crew of two, although a third occupant could be accommodated in the fuselage between the other two when required.

Seen in 1938 or 1939 with an under-wing bomb pannier clearly evident, L2649 was a 14 Squadron machine as witnessed by their motif – a winged plate and cross – on the fin, the unit having re-equipped with Wellesleys in March 1938 in the Middle East. Later transferred to 47 Squadron, L2649 subsequently joined the Khartoum Communication Flight prior to being SOC on 31 March 1943. (*Tony O'Toole collection*)

The part-obscured serial number suggests that this Wellesley is probably L2701 which served with 14, 223 and 47 Squadrons in the Middle East before being SOC on 31 December 1942. In this view the rear gunner's canopy is in the 'up' position which in flight shielded him and his gun from the worst effects of the aircraft's slipstream; unfortunately it also served as an effective but unintended airbrake that knocked several knots off the bomber's top speed. In order to supplement the Wellesley's meagre defensive fire, some mounted a second gun in the dorsal position and perhaps in the waist too, although its field of fire would have been somewhat limited.

Re-formed in Kenya in December 1936, 223 Squadron transferred to the Sudan in September 1939 from where it launched its first operation against the Italians on 11 June 1940; one day after Mussolini had decided it was safe to rush to the aid of his victorious German ally. Having received Wellesleys in June 1938, it is not clear whether the squadron was allocated a pre-war unit code prior to receiving the code 'AO' after 3 September 1939. Unidentified Wellesley 'AO-K' is seen here in 1940 with bombs lying beneath it, but note the stacked tins to the right of this picture, each bearing the word 'Shell' and the company logo. Susceptible to damage and easily ruptured, such flimsy petrol tins would later be replaced by reverse-engineered 'jerry cans'.

Seen here in a fighter-like pose, the Fairey Battle light bomber was impressive by the standards of 1936; an aircraft which at first glance appeared to own some of the attributes of the modern fighters then beginning to appear on the scene. K4303, the prototype Battle, first flew in March 1936 after an order for 155 (the first of 2,184) had already been placed, and trials later in the year with the A&AEE confirmed that the prototype met the necessary performance requirements outlined in the specification. Judged to be satisfactory as a light bomber when the first production examples entered RAF service with 63 Squadron in May 1937, such was the speed of progress that by September 1939 it was totally obsolete. Hopelessly outclassed by German Bf 109s and highly vulnerable to light flak, Battles were decimated over France in the spring of 1940. (*Tony Buttler collection*)

Streamlined and powered by a Merlin engine, it is easy to appreciate why the Battle appeared to offer great potential and why much was expected of it. However, it wasn't to be. The Battle was much larger than contemporary fighters, yet relied on virtually the same engine as the Spitfire to pull it through the sky complete with a crew of three, fuel and bomb load. The following data illustrates the differences: Battle, empty weight c 6,647lb (Spitfire I, empty, 4,306lb); Battle, maximum take-off weight 11,700lb (Spitfire I, loaded, 5,935lb); Battle, wingspan 54ft (Spitfire I span 36ft 10in); Battle, length 42ft 4in (Spitfire I, length 29ft 11in). These figures assume a 1,030hp Merlin III engine for both bomber and fighter alike. The Spitfire I's top speed hovered around the 360 mph mark depending on the combination of engine and propeller fitted. The Battle's top speed was a respectable 257 mph at 15,000ft reducing to c 210 mph at sea level, although realistically its cruising speed at 15,000ft with a 1,000lb bomb load, guns, ammunition and fuel was 147 mph. What this translated to at low level with an additional 500lb bomb load on external racks is hard to determine. Little wonder that the Battle proved too slow and unwieldy to survive daylight attacks against a well-organized and efficient enemy while employing outdated tactics.

Battles from 12 Squadron as seen in 1938 devoid of any unit markings, two of which are fitted with under-wing bomb carriers. When required, the Battle could carry up to 500lb of bombs externally in addition to the 1,000lb carried internally in under-wing cells located outboard of the undercarriage. Usually four 250lb general-purpose bombs were carried, one in each of the four cells; presumably four semi-armour-piercing (SAP) bombs would have been carried when used on anti-submarine patrols.

An all-too-familiar scene where the Battle was concerned after their decimation over the Low Countries in May 1940. However, this photo is deceptive inasmuch as L5451 'PH-C', a 12 Squadron machine, had made a forced landing while operating from its home base, Binbrook in Lincolnshire, in October 1940. Repaired, L5451 was transferred to Canada in February 1941.

Following the battle for France and the tragedies that had befallen their crews, surviving Battles were quickly removed from daylight bombing operations; however, the bomber was not immediately removed from all operational activities. Several were used to carry out night-time raids against troops, landing craft and barges congregating at Channel ports in preparation for the invasion of Britain. While the last bombing sorties to be made by RAF Battles occurred on 15/16 October 1940 when they attacked Boulogne and Calais, others were usefully employed on reconnaissance patrols along Northern Ireland's coast into 1941. Ultimately, Iceland-based 98 Squadron, a Coastal Command unit, became the last squadron to use the Battle operationally, the type being supplemented with Hurricane Is in June 1941 until the squadron disbanded a month later at which point the unit became 1423 Flight. Equipped with ten Hurricanes and two Battles, the Flight provided protection for Reykjavik as well escorting HMS *Prince of Wales* (carrying Winston Churchill) as the Prime Minister passed through Icelandic waters.

Handley Page HP.52 K4240 was a twin-engined, narrow-fuselage mid-wing monoplane which first flew in June 1936 and became the prototype Hampden bomber. In a much-modified form, production Hampdens are most often recalled as being one of Bomber Command's trio of night-bombers alongside the Wellington and Whitley during the earlier years of the war. The numeral '8' was applied for the 1936 Society of British Aircraft Constructors show held at Hatfield. (In 1964 its name was amended to become the Society of British Aerospace Companies).

Hampden production line: the narrowness of the type's fuselage is readily apparent. Without its wings it is easy to understand why they were dubbed, among other soubriquets, the 'Flying Suitcase' and the 'Flying Panhandle'.

Hampdens nearing completion c September 1939. Powered by two 1,000hp Bristol Pegasus XVIII engines, the bomber had a top speed of 254 mph and a cruising speed of 167 mph at 15,000ft. Bomb loads were restricted less by weight than the restrictions imposed by their narrow fuselage and bomb bay which usually accommodated four 500lb bombs, with two more carried externally if a drag penalty was accepted; alternatively, two 2,000lb high-capacity bombs could be carried internally. Able to accommodate mines, the Hampden was adapted to lay them in coastal waters, while others were later modified to carry an 18in torpedo. For defence the type relied on one (later two) rear-facing Vickers 'K' guns in each dorsal and ventral position with another in the nose. In addition, a single fixed 'fighter-style' Browning .303 machine gun was provided for the pilot. However, as would soon become apparent during the daylight raids against Germany, the Hampden's chances of defending itself were poor at best.

The Hampden was certainly narrow, as indicated by this view of the pilot's cockpit, the pilot having a firing button on the control column for his single fixed gun.

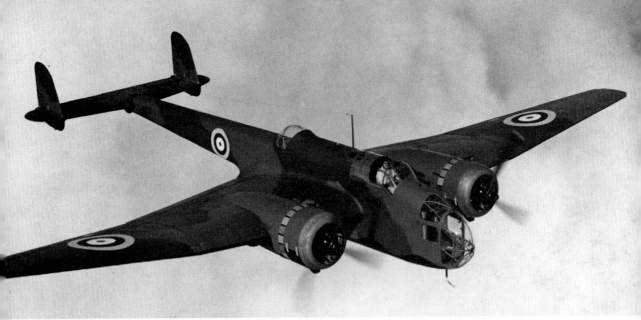

Occasionally miscaptioned as L4032 – the latter being the first production Hampden to fly (in June 1938) – this is in fact L4159. Its serial number is visible on the rear fuselage. (*Tony Buttler collection*)

L4159, seen from another angle, with part of its serial number visible below the wing in 1938 or 1939. Later delivered to 7 Squadron, L4159 was written off after it crashed into trees at Upper Heyford on 6 November 1939.

Hampden I L4115 at rest. Two Hampdens, L4032 and X3115, were fitted with 1100hp Wright Cyclone engines and designated as the Hampden Mk II, but the type never went into production and X3115 was later converted to become a Hampden TB.I torpedo-bomber. As for L4115, it was one of a batch of 180 delivered between August 1938 and June 1939 and served with 61 and 44 Squadrons plus 16 OTU prior to being converted to a TB.I. It was written off following a crash-landing on 1 May 1943 when serving with 5 OTU.

An unidentified Hampden seen during the pre-war months. The fuselage code 'LS' was allocated to 61 Squadron in February 1939 and retained until September when it changed to 'QR'.

Unidentified Hampdens from 61 Squadron wearing the code 'QR' which it used from September 1939 and throughout the war.

A Hampden climbs out of Radlett, Hertfordshire as a heavy freight train hauled by an LMS Beyer Garratt 2-6-0+0-6-2 passes the airfield. This Hampden, thought to be L4155, was photographed early in 1939 prior to being issued to 7 Squadron which relinquished its Whitley IIIs from April. Unfortunately L4155 didn't survive for long as it spun into the ground near Newark-on-Trent on 23 May that year.

A 49 Squadron Hampden being loaded with a mixture of 500lb and 250lb general-purpose (GP) bombs, some of which are for other aircraft. The GP bomb was a disappointing weapon; it suffered from an over-thick casing and, consequently, a low explosive charge-to-weight ratio of less than 30 per cent, which translated into relatively minimal blast damage and imperfect fragmentation as they tended to break up into large lumps rather than masses of much smaller but equally lethal fragments. Used throughout the war, they were supplemented from 1943 by the thinner-cased medium-capacity (MC) bomb which had a charge-to-weight ratio of 51 per cent. Although 250lb MC bombs were produced, they proved too small to be truly effective whereas the 500lb MCs – not to mention their heavier brethren – were.

Hampden P1333 'EA-F' is seen here in August 1940 at RAF Scampton, by which time the dorsal gun position had been fitted with twin Vickers 'K' machine guns. P1333 failed to return from an operation a few nights later on 16/17 August.

A variant of the Hampden was the Hereford. Powered by two 1,000hp 16-cylinder Napier Dagger in-line engines, the latter became notorious for continually overheating and in turn proved to be the cause of the Hereford's downfall. Just nine, all assigned to a flight of 185 Squadron, entered operational service but were soon withdrawn and thereafter most were allocated to training units. Engines apart, the Hereford was in almost every respect a Hampden; indeed, of the 150 Herefords ordered, approximately 20 were later converted to add to the 1,430 Hampdens built. Seen here is Hereford L6067, one of a batch of 100 delivered from August 1939, which was operated by 16 OTU until it crashed on 1 August 1940. (*Tony Buttler collection*)

With the exception of the Blenheim, all of the bombers referred to thus far may fairly be described as the RAF's forgotten bombers, but not so the Vickers Wellington which, while not quite as famous as the Hurricane and Spitfire, has, for good reason, received significant coverage elsewhere. Hence to avoid undue repetition, the Wellington's coverage, as per the two fighters, is brief.

This image of the Vickers-Armstrong factory, Weybridge, as seen on 6 July 1939, exposes the Wellington's geodetic method of construction. At the very back of the shop substantially complete Wellingtons are visible, one of which is a Wellington II fitted with Merlin engines as opposed to Pegasus radials. Proven to be the best of the RAF's pre-war twin-engined bombers, the Wellington, or 'Wimpey', became the backbone of the night attacks against Germany prior to the arrival of the four-engined bombers and remained operational with Bomber Command until early in October 1943.

The nearest airframes are Wellington Is, identified by the Vickers turrets arrayed in front of them, a design in which the upper (glazed) half of the turret remained fixed with only the track-mounted Browning .303 machine guns being able to traverse to either side. Despite reports that the Wellington I and IA were only fitted for but not with ventral 'dustbin' turrets, photographic evidence exists to prove that at least some were so fitted, with Mk IA N3000 'WS-L' being one example. With the introduction of the Wellington IA, Nash and Thompson (FN) turrets replaced the troublesome Vickers design in both nose and tail positions.

Displaying their squadron badge inset with its bat motif, the unit's motto translated reads 'Throughout the night we fly'. Having received its first Wellingtons in January 1939, this well-known image shows 9 Squadron's Wellington Is in loose formation a few weeks later when, nominally at least, they still 'owned' a few Heyford IIIs, the last of which were flown away in May. L4274 'KA-K' went on to serve with the Central Gunnery School and 3 Blind (later Beam) Approach Training Flight prior to being written off on 28 August 1941 following an in-flight fire. The code 'KA' changed to 'WS' after the outbreak of war, by which time the unit was in the process of receiving the Mk IA.

Another early Wellington unit was 115 Squadron which began replacing its Harrows with the Wellington I from March 1939. The process was completed by June, although they in turn would be replaced by more battleworthy Mk IAs from September. To prove the point that not every unit code changed overnight on 3/4 September, 115 Squadron's pre-war code 'BK' was retained into November when it was replaced by 'KO'. Wellington I L4221 'BK-U' went on to serve with 3 General Reconnaissance Unit when it formed in April 1940 with three, later five, Wellington DWIs. (Reportedly, L4221 was one of the DWI prototypes.) (*Carl Vincent via Tony O'Toole*)

An unidentified Wellington DWI: if not the rarest mark of Wellington, then certainly the easiest to identify. By late 1939, German magnetic mines were posing a serious threat to ships entering the estuaries and entrances to British harbours. They would lay dormant until triggered by the magnetic field of a passing vessel which, if sufficiently close to the seat of the explosion, would either be sunk outright or receive damage sufficient for it to be deemed a constructive total loss fit only for scrapping.

In due course a magnetic mine was recovered and examined. Accordingly a ship-degaussing programme was devised whereby a vessel's magnetic field was neutralized and the Royal Navy developed minesweepers capable of dealing with the threat, all of which took time. Hence a Wellington was set aside equipped with an auxiliary engine in the fuselage and an external 48ft-diameter magnetic coil. When energized it was hoped that a powerful magnetic field could be generated that was sufficient to detonate a magnetic mine while the aircraft was flying high enough and fast enough to escape any resulting explosion unharmed. It worked. Designated Wellington DWI (Directional Wireless Installation: a term intended to deceive enemy intelligence), only a handful were completed.

Wellington IC R1041 seen here in 1940. As evident, the original fixed Vickers-type gun turret in the nose (and tail) have been replaced by more effective twin-gun Nash and Thompson FN5A turrets, fitted front and rear, to the Wellington IA and IC.

The Bristol Type 130 was designed in the early/mid-1930s as a replacement for the ageing biplane Vickers Valentia bomber-transport then in service with the RAF in the Middle East, where their ability to convey troops and stretcher cases over long distances made them an indispensable asset. K3583, the prototype Type 130, first flew on 23 June 1935 and in April 1937 the Air Ministry ordered eighty (later reduced to fifty) modified airframes to be known as the Bristol Bombay.

Seen at Hendon in 1935 with attendant ground crew displaying what appears to be 'AA' Automobile Association logos on their coveralls, the prototype displays its original front gun position and wheel spats to advantage, although neither would be fitted to production machines. Having suffered an undercarriage failure while taxiing in 1939, K3583 was returned to the manufacturer who retained the prototype for development work and named her 'Josephine'. (*Tony Buttler collection*)

Does the Bombay belong in the bomber section? It was never an interim bomber as was the Harrow, despite both being ordered as bomber-transports. Primarily this was due to the Harrow having entered service early enough to play a part in the expansion of Bomber Command at a critical time, while the Bombay didn't enter operational service until late in 1939. By then, with modern bombers established in service, a disturbing shortage of transport aircraft for use at home and abroad was apparent; consequently it was to the Middle East that the majority of Bombays were sent for use as transports, their original *raison d'être*. In the event, however, following Italy's declaration of war in June 1940, they were frequently used as night-bombers for many months. In fact L5816, seen here in 1939, later joined 216 Squadron in Egypt but failed to return from a night raid against Benghazi on 19 October 1940. Thus, tenuously perhaps, the type is included here. (*Tony O'Toole collection*)

The first production Bombay, L5808, made its first flight in March 1939 and was allocated to the A&AEE until it was damaged beyond repair in August 1939. The first operational examples were allocated to 216 Squadron in Egypt where they arrived in October 1939. Ultimately 216 Squadron went on to operate no fewer than thirty-seven of the fifty constructed at various times before the last was replaced by Douglas Dakotas in 1943. The Bombay could accommodate 2,000lb of bombs (carried internally and externally), had a maximum speed of 192 mph and a normal operating range of 880 miles with a ferry range of 2,200 miles.

The last Bombay to emerge wearing overall silver dope was L5818, seen here, which was allocated to 10 FTS but didn't survive for long. Poor weather was the cause of a forced landing near Stafford on 10 October 1939, resulting in L5818 being written off. (*Tony Buttler collection*)

Bombay L5838 seen in late 1939/40 prior to joining 216 Squadron in Egypt, its single gun being just visible in the forward turret. Usually this would be a Vickers 'K' (mounted on its side) with a second in the tail turret; a feeble armament often augmented by two further guns mounted one on each beam. When operating as a transport a crew of three was generally sufficient; as a bomber carrying eight 250lb bombs, four was usual. However, when a load of ninety 20lb bombs was carried, then a crew of five was advisable. Carried internally, each bomb was passed by hand along the fuselage and had its arming vane safety wire cut by a crewman. He then passed it to the man nearest the door who threw them out by hand!

Having served with 216 Squadron, L5838 was passed to the Khartoum Communication Flight before joining 1 Air Ambulance Unit, RAAF, with which it served until damaged beyond repair on 27 July 1943 at Philippeville, Algeria. The last Bombays were withdrawn in August 1944. (*Tony Buttler collection*)

A 216 Squadron Bombay seen in the Middle East during 1940. Most RAF units tended to use fuselage roundels to separate a unit code from the airframe's individual identity letter, but as can be seen here, 216 Squadron tended to group theirs together at this time, hence 'SHA' with 'SH' representing the unit code. (*Tony O'Toole collection*)

Chapter Three

The Searchers: Maritime Patrol

Coastal Command didn't fare particularly well in the pre-war acquisition of modern and effective aircraft. True, limited numbers of the four-engined Short Sunderland flying boat were available by September 1939 and the Command could boast several squadrons of Avro Ansons which, as a weapon of war, could only really be described as barely adequate. Even so, Ansons would provide much useful service during the first eighteen months of the war, which, in the case of at least one Coastal Command unit, stretched into 1942. In addition, several Bristol Blenheim IF fighters were allocated to the Command for North Sea patrol duties.

A new type, the twin-engined Bristol Beaufort bomber/torpedo-bomber, would eventually become operational in April 1940, allowing the last of the obsolete Vickers Vildebeest biplanes to be replaced. Despite being plagued initially by engine failures, the Beaufort proved to be a good aircraft, one destined to mature and perform well in the years ahead, unlike the Blackburn Botha. The latter, intended to supplement the Beaufort was, alas, woeful and the few that did eventually enter service in 1940 were soon withdrawn from operational duties and replaced by Ansons, one of the types the Botha was intended to replace.

It was indeed fortunate, therefore, that for the general reconnaissance (maritime reconnaissance) role, quantities of US-built Lockheed Hudsons were procured to supplement Coastal Command's existing maritime patrol aircraft which, Anson and Sunderland apart, included several units equipped with obsolete London, Singapore and Stranraer biplane flying boats.

At the outbreak of hostilities, Coastal Command's sole front-line torpedo-bomber force consisted of 22 and 42 Squadrons based at Thorney Island and Bircham Newton respectively. Both were equipped with the Vickers Vildebeest biplane torpedo-bomber which in its Mk I form had been introduced into RAF service in late 1932. By 1939, both units were operating the three-seat Mk III and Mk IV, although a quantity of elderly two-seat Mk Is were re-issued to 22 Squadron in September 1939. This 1930/31 image shows prototype 'Vildebeeste' Mk I wearing the manufacturer's number 'N230'. In 1934 the name was amended slightly to Vildebeest. (*Newark Air Museum*)

Vildebeest III K4157 '16' served with 22 Squadron for a few months in 1935, although it is uncertain whether this photo was taken while serving with them or whether it was while serving with 'N' Flight at Gosport in 1936. K4157 suffered an accident at Gosport in August 1936 and was later SOC. (*Tony O'Toole collection*)

A requirement for torpedo-bomber squadrons to defend Singapore resulted in 100 Squadron leaving Scotland for Seletar in 1933 where it joined the similarly-equipped 36 Squadron. Leaving its Vildebeest Is behind, 100 Squadron operated two-seat Mk IIs from August 1933 until December 1941 and three-seat Mk IIIs from December 1937 to February 1942 when most were destroyed by the advancing Japanese. Seen here is Vildebeest II K2927 '9' from 100 Squadron at Seletar between 1934 and 19 March 1936, the day it crashed into the sea during a practice torpedo drop. (*Newark Air Museum*)

Having entered service in 1936 the Avro Anson soon became ubiquitous; an aircraft usually associated with air crew training, light transport, communications and general duties. So useful was the Anson that later marks continued to serve the RAF until 1968 when the last, a C.19, was finally retired. However, despite its limitations and small bomb load, the Anson I provided Coastal Command with a useful coastal patrol aircraft at a time when other types were in very short supply. Given the vast areas the Command was expected to patrol, they enabled longer-ranging flying boats and Hudsons to be released to cover more distant areas.

This image shows unidentified Anson I 'KQ-E' from 502 Squadron which as a body transferred to Coastal Command on 28 November 1938, transitioning from Hinds to Ansons in the process. In September their code changed to 'YG' and the unit was sent to patrol off the Irish coast, retaining them until replaced by Whitleys from October 1940, during which time the unit also trialled the Blackburn Botha! (*Tony O'Toole collection*)

Influenced by and evolved from the Blenheim, the Bristol Beaufort was a twin-engined bomber, torpedo-bomber and general reconnaissance aircraft with a crew of four; the first operational examples going to 22 Squadron Coastal Command in November 1939. Unfortunately, extensive service trials were then required to overcome serious unreliability issues associated with their Bristol Taurus sleeve-valve radial engines which delayed their operational debut until April. April 1940 also saw the introduction of the Beaufort I to 42 Squadron, allowing the RAF to finally retire its home-based Vildebeests from front-line service.

L4441, a prototype Beaufort, made the type's initial flight on 15 October 1938, it and seventy-seven others having been ordered off the drawing board in August 1936. L4441 to L4115 were all classed as non-standard airframes and considered to be prototypes. (*Tony Buttler collection*)

Displaying its original curved bomb-aimer's window, L4441 is seen in 1938 after its undercarriage fairing plates had been removed. Following service with test establishments, it became a test-bed trialling various modifications intended to make the Taurus more reliable and less prone to overheating. Later issued to 5 OTU, L4441 was damaged in a forced landing on 12 October 1941 and grounded.

Beaufort I W6498 'AW-K' belonging to 42 Squadron is seen here in 1941, its individual identity letter 'K' having been modified to read 'Killer'. Delivered to 42 Squadron between December 1940 and March 1941, Killer had a long life by wartime standards, surviving the war to be SOC on 27 September 1945 following service with 42, 143 and 217 Squadrons as well as 2 and 9 OTU.

Allocated to 32 OTU, RCAF, Beaufort I L9967 'K' shows its optically-flat bomb-aimer's windscreens and just about reveals the code 'OP' on the rear fuselage, not to be confused with 11 OTU, RAF which used the same code. Confusion is averted because 32 OTU formed at Liverpool on 20 July 1941 and embarked for Canada the following day (although its Beauforts didn't arrive until the end of the year).

It is sometimes argued that the Beaufort's maximum bomb load was 1,650lb – i.e. the weight of a torpedo – when in fact it could lift 2,000lb, the weight of the armour-piercing (AP) bomb shown here. Impressive-looking, the bomb had two flaws. The first lay in the difficulties encountered in trying to hit a target with a single bomb from the altitudes required for it to gain sufficient velocity to penetrate deck armour. Secondly, its robust body accounted for 91 per cent of its weight, rendering the explosive charge a little too weak to create the internal havoc desired; a balancing act also encountered by the designers of AP shells used by contemporary battleships and cruisers. That said, kinetic energy also has a part to play in these things, as was discovered by the crew of battleship *Gneisenau* when at least one 2,000lb AP bomb hit home on 26/27 February 1942. (*Carl Vincent via Tony O'Toole*)

Two 42 Squadron Beaufort Is displaying differences in camouflage and armament. The nearest, N1172 'AW-S', was delivered c September 1940 and was lost during a strike on enemy shipping in April 1942, while L9834 – delivered in mid-1940 – was lost in an accident on 30 August 1941. The armament carried by RAF Beauforts varied with time, albeit never with anything heftier than the .303 machine gun. They entered service with one, later two, fixed Browning machine guns in their wings that were later supplemented by or replaced by two gimbal-mounted Vickers 'K' guns in the nose. Initially the dorsal turret carried one and later two Vickers 'K' guns, replaced in later turrets by twin Brownings, often augmented by two beam-mounted Vickers 'K' guns firing from ports forward of the turret. Some were also fitted with a rear-firing Browning mounted in a blister beneath the nose, as seen on 'AW-S' albeit often soon removed. (*Tony Buttler collection*)

The Blackburn Botha, a twin-engined torpedo-bomber and general reconnaissance aircraft, was one of the types chosen to re-equip Coastal Command along with the Beaufort I and Saro (SAunders-ROe) Lerwick, of which only the Beaufort could be considered successful. Issued first to 608 Squadron in June 1940, Bothas made their first operational patrol on 10 August 1940 and their last on 6 November, forcing 608 to revert to using Ansons. No. 502 Squadron received three Bothas in August 1940, but within weeks Whitleys had arrived and the Bothas were despatched to an OTU. Seen here is Botha L6264 which served with 8 B&GS and 10 AOS prior to being reported missing during a night exercise in October 1941. (*Tony Buttler collection*)

As poor as the handful of Saro Lerwicks would prove to be, the Botha was worse, despite which 582 of them were built. Seriously underpowered with numerous other shortcomings, their numbers ensured that a use had to be found for them. Perversely they were issued to numerous training establishments which used them to train pilots, observers, navigators, radio-operators and gunners. Declared obsolete in 1943, the last examples were finally grounded in 1944. This image of an unidentified Botha shows its FN7 dorsal turret and two Browning .303 machine guns to good effect. A single fixed .303 machine gun was provided for the pilot. Bothas were powered by two Bristol Perseus radial engines and could carry up to 2,000lb of bombs or a single torpedo. (*Tony Buttler collection*)

The Lockheed Hudson, a twin-engined maritime and general reconnaissance monoplane, was the first American-built aircraft to see operational service with the RAF in the Second World War, the first of which were just entering service with Coastal Command when hostilities began. As their numbers increased it allowed the Anson to be gradually removed from front-line operations and replaced by an aircraft better suited to patrolling the harsh maritime wastes. This particular aircraft, Hudson III T9456, was photographed prior to having its dorsal turret and nose guns fitted. Seemingly delivered to the RAF in May or June 1941, T9456 was allocated to 269 Squadron then engaged on anti-U-boat patrol duties at Kaldadarnes, Iceland. However, T9456 is in fact recorded as having been cannibalized for spares there following a landing accident on 28 April 1941!

The RAF operated several types of flying boat between the wars, often procured in penny-packet quantities which, nevertheless, certainly helped to protect the UK's maritime interests. By 1936, a few familiar names such as the Blackburn Perth, Saro Cloud, Short Rangoon and Supermarine Southampton still lingered on until finally withdrawn in 1937/1938. Hopefully, the single image of a Southampton flying boat will suffice to illustrate the RAF's inter-war flying boat era, although in truth they were perhaps not so far removed from the biplane flying boats that did remain operational in September 1939!

Supermarine Southampton II S1229 was one of eight still in service in 1936, mostly with the Seaplane Training Squadron. A few wooden-hulled Southampton Is entered RAF service in mid-1925, but were succeeded by the Mk II featuring an anodically treated duralumin hull which was lighter than wood and didn't suffer from water soakage as did the Mk I, the two factors combining to make the Mk II more than 900lb lighter than its predecessor. With a span of 75ft and powered by two Napier Lion V engines, the Southampton II had a top speed of 108 mph at sea level. Able to carry 1,100lb of bombs, for defence it relied on three Lewis guns located in the bow and two beam positions; the latter were offset so that both could engage an enemy sitting below or almost directly aft of the tailplane. S1229 served until December 1936, while the last (believed to be S1228) was withdrawn c March 1937.

Originally to be called the Supermarine Southampton IV, its name was changed to Scapa in 1933 as a result of the many differences that existed between it and the Southampton II. The prototype, S1648 seen here, first flew in July 1932 and was followed by fourteen production Scapas, many of which remained in service until replaced by Singapores in late 1938. Several survived into 1939 with two still 'on the books' in August 1940; however, this does not imply that they were in any sense operational or even flyable given that a few were retained, minus their engines, and used to train seaplane-tender crews in the art of towing flying boats. Scapas had a maximum speed of 141 mph at 3,200ft, a wingspan of 75ft and were powered by two RR Kestrel IIIMS engines. Scapas carried the same bomb load and number of guns as the Southampton II.

The prototype Saro London, K3560, first flew in April 1934 with production airframes entering operational service with 201 Squadron two years later. Described as a general-purpose coastal reconnaissance flying boat, Londons proved to be robust and reliable. Thirty production Londons were built, all but one of which survived to serve in the Second World War. Here K3560 displays its polygonal cowlings which, for a time, distinguished it and thirteen production Mk Is from the seventeen Mk IIs that were also procured until the former were converted to Mk II standard in 1937/38. K3560 effectively became the prototype Mk II when its original Bristol Pegasus III engines were replaced by the Pegasus X driving four-bladed propellers. K3560 was SOC in March 1939.

Issued to 228 Squadron in February 1937, London I K5258 later served with the Marine Aircraft Experimental Establishment (MAEE) until it was returned to Saro in September 1938 for conversion to Mk II standard prior to joining 240 Squadron in June 1939. Londons carried the 'standard' RAF biplane flying boat armament of three Lewis guns located one each in bow, amidships and stern positions, which at least allowed the crew of K5258 to throw something back when attacked by Heinkel 111s on 19 December 1939. Allocated to BOAC on 1 August 1940, K5258 was SOC on 31 December 1941. (*Newark Air Museum*)

A converted Mk I camouflaged 240 Squadron London II K5910 'BN-L' was photographed *c* mid-1940 prior to being allocated to BOAC in August. Upon its return to RAF service, K5910 served with 4 OTU before being sent to Felixstowe in August 1942 for dismantling. The type's last operational patrol was made by 202 Squadron's K5911 on 4 June 1941, although several continued to serve with the Flying Boat Training Squadron (FBTS) and 4 OTU into 1942. The last survivors, perhaps five in number, had all been returned to Saro by 13 November 1942 for breaking up. (*Newark Air Museum*)

A Short Singapore Mk III. Derived from the Singapore II which didn't enter production, Shorts built four aircraft to a modified design to be trialled by the MAEE and 210 Squadron, the latter also serving to ferry flying boats abroad. Named Singapore III, the first, K3592, made its first flight on 15 June 1934 with all four initially serving as trials aircraft. The type entered operational service in April 1935 with 205 and 230 Squadrons, later followed by 203, 209, 228 and finally 240 Squadron in November 1938. In addition to the original four, thirty-three others were procured with the last being delivered in June 1937. Powered by four Kestrel engines (two tractor and two pusher), the Singapore III weighed 18,400lb empty, about the same as a London's loaded weight. The latter had a wingspan of 80ft compared to the Singapore III's 90ft span and each could carry up to 2,000lb of bombs. As per the London, Singapore IIIs carried three Lewis guns for defence.

First flown on 24 July 1934, K3593 went to 210 Squadron for service trials prior to joining 205 Squadron at Seletar in April 1935 where this photo was taken. An ace of spades appears below the cockpit with the hilt of a kris dagger superimposed; a kris appears on 205 Squadron's badge and originates from their association with Malaya. K3593 was SOC in March 1938. (*Newark Air Museum*)

Singapore III K4577 as seen at Felixstowe in mid-1935 while being used for armament and equipment trials, which probably explains the presence of the containers beneath the wing which are very close to if not actually on the waterline. A Lewis gun is mounted in the nose with a pan of ammunition in place. By October 1935, K4577 was with 203 Squadron in Aden where it served until SOC in January 1940 after which it was moored out to act as a decoy. (*Newark Air Museum*)

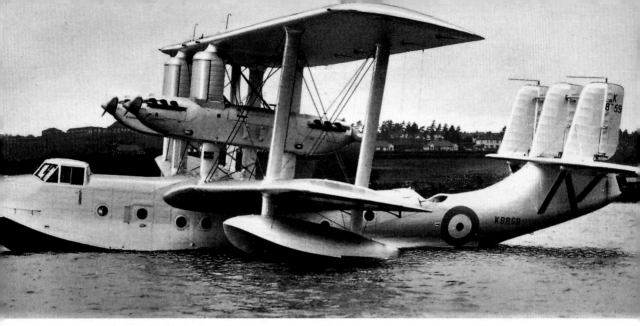

The last Singapore III to be built, K8859, was delivered to 210 Squadron on 9 June 1937. Subsequently, it was ferried to Iraq in October 1937 for onward delivery to 203 Squadron, its departure from the UK having been delayed while damage was repaired following a forced landing the previous August. Later transferred to 205 Squadron at Seletar, K8859 was SOC on 20 February 1941. (*Newark Air Museum*)

An unidentified Singapore III '7', but possibly K3594 from 205 Squadron. By the start of the Second World War, only 203 and 205 Squadrons in the Middle and Far East respectively were still flying these impressive but elderly flying boats. No. 203 Squadron relinquished theirs in March 1940, although at least four were subsequently moored out as floating decoys, while 205 continued to use theirs operationally until October 1941. Even then four were transferred to the Royal New Zealand Air Force who operated them at Suda Bay, Fiji until April 1943. All told it appears that at least nineteen Singapore IIIs remained extant when war broke out, with some, as related, remaining operational abroad while others in the UK served non-operationally with the MAEE, FBTS and 4 OTU into 1941. (*Newark Air Museum*)

The Supermarine Stranraer was the last multi-engined biplane flying boat to enter RAF service. The prototype seen here, K3973, originally known as the Southampton V, made its first flight in July 1934, albeit its name was changed a month later. Seventeen production Stranraers followed, with the first, K7287, joining 228 Squadron in April 1937 where it began the gradual process of replacing the unit's existing complement of Scapas, Londons and Singapores. No. 228 Squadron received its first Short Sunderland I in November 1938 but retained Stranraers until April 1939. The second Stranraer unit, 209 Squadron, operated them from December 1938 until April 1940 alongside the ill-fated Saro Lerwick. The RAF's only other operational Stranraer unit, 240 Squadron, began replacing its Londons with the 'new' biplane in June 1940 and retained them until April 1941. Reportedly, the last operational patrol by an RAF Stranraer was carried out by K7287 'BN-B' from 240 Squadron on 26 February 1941. Otherwise, a few continued in use with 4 OTU throughout 1941, of which two survived until late 1942, namely K7295 – damaged beyond repair on 4 September at Loch Ness – and K7303 (the last RAF Stranraer built), which was finally SOC by 4 OTU on 31 October 1942.

Stranraers had a wingspan of 85ft, were powered by two 920hp Pegasus X engines, carried a 1,000lb bomb load and were provided with three Lewis guns for self-defence.

Lest you wonder why the author keeps referring to RAF Stranraers, it is to differentiate from the forty built by Canadian Vickers Ltd for the RCAF. Used from 1938 and throughout the war, the Canadians found them to be more seaworthy than the Consolidated Canso (Catalina in RAF terminology) monoplane flying boats which they also used. These two images show Stranraer 912 on land and afloat, the code 'FY-A' being allocated to 4 Squadron RCAF from August 1939 to May 1942. (*Both images: Carl Vincent via Tony O'Toole*)

Hopefully the preceding images of biplane flying boats will help to emphasize the visual transformation presented by the (almost) sudden appearance of the big four-engined monoplane flying boat, an apparent leap from the seemingly archaic to something far more modern in appearance. In its own way, the transition from a Southampton or Singapore to a Sunderland carried with it a similar degree of dramatic impact for the average citizen in 1937 as did the transition from the Fury biplane to the Hurricane.

This image shows Short Sunderland prototype K4774 following its first flight on 16 October 1937. Broadly a development of the civil Short C-Class Empire flying boats, the first of which had flown in July 1936, K4774 was allocated to the MAEE in April 1938 with which it remained until SOC in 1944. Originally fitted with four 950hp Pegasus X radial engines, these were later replaced by 1,010hp Pegasus XXIIs.

The RAF's first Sunderland order ran to eleven airframes which were delivered between April and August 1938, with forty-two either available or awaiting delivery by September 1939. The first production airframe L2158, seen here, initially served with the MAEE before joining 204 Squadron who operated it until 17 August 1942 when it went missing while escorting a convoy near Sierra Leone. Mark Is were powered by four Pegasus XXII engines, could lift a 2,000lb bomb load and carried a single Vickers 'K' gun in a power-operated FN11 nose turret with two more on pillar mounts in dorsal hatches aft of the wing. A power-operated FN13 turret with four .303 Brownings was fitted in the tail position giving the Mk I – the version seen here – a total of seven guns. (*Tony Buttler collection*)

<u>Sunderland conundrum: how many guns did they carry?</u> While the Sunderland I's defensive armament has been noted above, much has been said elsewhere about the number of guns carried by later marks, notably the III and V. Third-party remarks reveal 'up to eighteen', but always as virtual throwaway comments without explanation. Other than Sunderlands used in weapons trials, the number appears to be a maximum of twelve .303 machine guns, mounted two each in the nose and dorsal turrets, four in the tail, and four fixed nose-mounted weapons for the pilot to suppress return fire from U-boats, particularly later in the war. Additionally, Sunderlands could also mount a .5in machine gun in each waist position, usually noted in post-war photos of the Mk V, although there is nothing to say that they were not fitted during the war. Thus the count appears to total twelve guns; fourteen if the .5in weapons are also included.

No. 210 Squadron Sunderland I L5798 'DA-A' is seen here almost at a point between wind and water on an unknown date. L5798 went on to serve with 201 and 204 Squadrons before being SOC on 20 September 1943 after suffering severe storm damage at Gibraltar. (*Newark Air Museum*)

Seen here on patrol in 1941, the weathered Sunderland I L2163 displays its gun positions including the two dorsal hatches; less easily noticed is the hinged bomb-aimer's window below the forward turret. At this time L2163 belonged to 210 Squadron as revealed by the letters 'DA' on the fuselage. It later went on to serve with 240 Squadron, 10 Squadron RAAF and 228 Squadron and remained operational until 15 January 1942 when it sank during a storm at Stranraer. Recovered, it served on as maintenance airframe 4891M. (*Tony Buttler collection*)

Intended to replace the London and Stranraer flying boats, the Saro Lerwick, once hopefully referred to as the 'baby Sunderland', was a great disappointment. Twenty-one of them, serial numbered L7248 to L7268, were built but the type suffered from an unstable hull design, a ferocious stall and several other unpleasant handling characteristics that were never cured. Powered by two 1,370hp Bristol Hercules II engines, the Lerwick had a wingspan of 80ft 10in, could carry eight 250lb depth-charges and was fitted with three power-operated turrets in nose, dorsal and tail positions with a single Vickers 'K' in the nose, two .303 Brownings in the dorsal turret and four in the tail.

This image shows the first of its type, L7248, after arriving for trials with the MAEE in March 1939, about four months after making its first flight. Seen from this angle it just about reveals its original 'small' fin and rudder. While still attached to the MAEE, L7248 dived into a hill near Faslane on 21 October 1941 after an engine failure. (*Tony Buttler collection*)

Believed to be Lerwick L7249, this aircraft is seen in mid-1939 after having had its fin and rudder enlarged in an attempt to cure some of the type's handling problems, although in effect it didn't help much and the Lerwick's handling remained unacceptable. L7249 sank while being launched at Felixstowe on 1 September 1939. Of the remaining nineteen airframes, seven sank, four crashed and one went missing in January 1941. The remaining seven were SOC shortly before being dismantled in late 1942. (*Tony Buttler collection*)

At least two Lerwicks joined 240 Squadron for service trials from July to September 1939, but the only RAF unit to use them operationally was 209 Squadron from December 1939 until May 1941, the survivors being sent to join 4 OTU which also used them. One might assume the OTU would discard them as soon as possible, but in fact they were retained long enough to be issued to the unfortunate Canadians of 422 Squadron when it formed at Loch Erne on 2 April 1942. Initially equipped with a single example, by August they had seven but whether they were ever used operationally seems doubtful given that the type had already been withdrawn from operational service and that 422 was instructed to fly them to Greenock in September 1942 to be broken up.

Seen here in early 1940 is Lerwick L7259 'WQ-F' of 209 Squadron wearing non-standard roundels for the period. A survivor of sorts, L7259 was operated by 209 Squadron, 4 OTU and then 422 Squadron as 'DG-Q' prior to being SOC on 29 November 1942. The last surviving example appears to have been L7254/3300M, which sank in Wig Bay on 10 December 1942. (*Tony Buttler collection*)

The specification for a long-range flying boat that had led to the Sunderland also produced a would-be competitor from Saunders Roe known as the Saro A.33. A large machine with a span of 95ft, it was powered by four 830hp Bristol Perseus XII engines and was intended to carry a 2,000lb bomb load and seven .303 machine guns in much the same configuration as the Sunderland I, although it is doubtful if any were ever fitted.

Completed in September 1938 and first flown on 14 October, it was quickly discovered that the A.33 suffered from a tendency to porpoise while taxiing, taking off and landing. Eleven days later, on 25 October 1938, while taking off in the Solent the aircraft hit a ferry's wake, causing it to bounce high in the air, stall and fall back onto the water, resulting in wing failure. Towed ashore, A.33 K4773 was found to be damaged beyond repair and development was thus halted, with the order for eleven further airframes cancelled. (*All from Tony Buttler collection*)

Chapter Four

General-Purpose, Army Co-Operation and Miscellaneous Duties

For years following the Second World War, books, magazines and documentaries fostered or sustained the impression, presumably by recalling wartime propaganda, that once war was declared, armadas of modern RAF monoplanes stood ready to 'ascend and darken the enemy sky'. In fact the message was far from the truth, as great armadas of British monoplanes didn't yet exist. By extension the message implied, or at least posed the underlying question, of what became of the RAF's mass of biplanes, because they *did* exist. The straight answer is nothing much; the majority were still there.

In fact entire fleets of obsolescent biplanes were in use when the war started; indeed, a few were still in use when the war finished! By late 1939, UK-based biplanes represented a valuable resource for the RAF despite their antiquity. Some, like the Gladiator, remained operational for want of Hurricanes and Spitfires; the Vildebeest had to be retained until sufficient Beauforts became available to replace it; and the Hector would operate against German forces near the Channel coast for want of (scarcely less vulnerable) Lysanders, while scores of others were needed for a host of subsidiary roles including use as airfield decoys or as ground instructional airframes.

In the Middle East biplanes remained very much in evidence. Most, having been equipped to carry guns and bombs in the first place, would continue to do so; their roles expanding from policing recalcitrant tribes in the region to conducting operations against Axis forces in Egypt, the Sudan, East Africa, Syria, Iraq and elsewhere until sufficient numbers of more modern types could finally be spared to replace them. Similarly, others remained active in training, transport and support roles, including spraying locust swarms.

Also in the Far East, in 1942, Vildebeest torpedo-bombers, Fairey Seals and even RNZAF Singapore flying boats faced the Japanese in the months following their attack on Pearl Harbor.

Hopefully this chapter will succeed in providing some visual interest with regard to the many types of aircraft that remained available to the RAF in 1939, and often well beyond. For ease of reference the aircraft featured in this section are presented alphabetically by manufacturer.

Avro Anson I L9145 from 267 Squadron is seen here at the 1940 Commanders-in-Chief Summit in the Middle East with an unidentified Wellesley from 47 Squadron (unit code 'KU') beyond. (*Tony O'Toole collection*)

Anson I L9155 from 24 Squadron, which re-formed in 1920 as a communications and training unit. Throughout the early war years the squadron operated an array of aircraft, both military and impressed civil types with which to carry out its duties. Photographed at Leconfield, Yorkshire in 1939, L9155 was SOC in August 1944.

Anson I N9832 'GL-G' belonged to 185 Squadron when this photo was taken during the winter of 1939. On 8 April 1940 the squadron merged into 14 OTU, training Hampden and Hereford crews at RAF Cottesmore. N9832 survived the transition and retained the code 'GL-G'. (*Tony O'Toole collection*)

An unknown Anson I, possibly from 4 FTS.

Armstrong Whitworth Whitley II K7262, long since removed from service as a bomber, was allocated to the Parachute Training School on 14 August 1940 and is seen here in May 1941 during a demonstration prepared for King George VI. K7262 was SOC on 7 August 1943. (*Tony Buttler collection*)

Fairey Battle L5664 'JQ-O', a target tug (TT) allocated to 2 AACU, is seen here in mid-1940. A wind-driven winch can be seen adjacent to the second crewman who operated the winch and associated target drogue, the latter carried in the fairing below the rear fuselage. As well as Battles, 2 AACU also used Gladiators, Rocs, Henleys and Hectors as target tugs in 1940/41. L5664 was allocated to the South African Air Force (SAAF) in June 1942.

Battle trainer R7365 from 12 FTS in 1940. Adaptable if nothing else, Fairey developed this pilot training variant in 1940 with individual cockpits because the original glazed canopy severely restricted the forward view of the rear occupant. The odd 'triangle' immediately ahead of the fin is a yellow gas warning panel. R7365 was allocated to the RCAF in June 1941.

The Fairey Seal was a naval spotter-reconnaissance design capable of carrying up to 500lb of bombs. Ninety-one were delivered from 1932, but despite being a Fleet Air Arm type, only two were passed to the Admiralty when it regained control of its air arm in March 1939. At least ten Seals survived to be allocated to the RAF's Number 10 Air Observers School on 3 September 1939 (becoming 10 B&GS on 1 January 1940), while four others were sent to Ceylon (Sri Lanka) in 1939. Returned to operational duty for want of anything better, they were still there in 1942 when the Japanese navy attacked. This image of Seal K3483 was taken while operating as a target tug with 10 AOS or 10 B&GS and was SOC on 30 October 1940.

Seen in 1943 or 1944, this immaculate and unidentified Gloster Gladiator was converted by Shorts of Belfast to undertake the unsung but vital meteorological reconnaissance role. Although no longer armed, this Gladiator's purposeful fighting biplane image remained as intense as ever. (*Tony O'Toole collection*)

Both this and the following image reflect the fact that, no matter how improbable it might seem, several of these elderly and vulnerable aircraft remained in harm's way right up until the end of the war. While most surviving Handley Page Harrows were used as transports with little alteration, others were taken in hand for a more extensive modification whereby gun positions were removed and replaced by extended fairings and often nicknamed 'Sparrows'. K6941 'BJ-K' was allocated to 271 Squadron on 25 September 1941 where it remained until SOC on 15 March 1945.

K6994's conversion to a 'Sparrow' commenced in September 1942, after which it was returned to 271 Squadron at RAF Tollerton retaining the code 'BJ-U'. Here, K6994 (by now marked 'U'), is seen on the ground in Normandy on 12 September 1944 wearing reduced D-Day identification stripes on the rear fuselage. Badly damaged by the Luftwaffe on 1 January 1945 at Evere, Belgium, where seven other Harrows were destroyed, K6994 was SOC six weeks later. It seems likely that the last surviving Harrow/Sparrow was K7000 which made its final flight at the end of April 1945 and was SOC on 1 June. Of related interest, a few Harrows had been used over southern England during the Blitz to sow aerial parachute mines (Operation MUTTON) in the projected path of Luftwaffe bombers; a desperate and potentially dangerous tactic given that twice, in December 1940 and March 1941, K6994 was damaged by the premature explosion of its own mines – which makes one wonder as to the lethality of the munition in the first place!

The Hawker Hart light bomber – as fast or indeed faster than some contemporary single-seat fighters when it entered operational service in February 1930 – became the basis of an entire family of aircraft that went on to equip the RAF in the 1930s. Largely replaced by Hinds in Bomber Command by mid-1936 and the Reserve and Auxiliary squadrons a little later, Harts continued to provide sterling service abroad, often operationally, and at home in various training and second-line capacities. Delivered in December 1930, K1418 is seen here while operating with India-based 11 Squadron at Risalpur (in modern-day Pakistan). Fitted with a replacement rudder donated by Hart K2126, K1418 survived until SOC following a forced landing in the Kabul River in May 1938.

K2090 was a Hart (India), a variant adapted for use in the hostile environment of the North-West Frontier. When photographed in the mid-1930s it belonged to 39 Squadron, who allocated it the individual identity '7'. Later transferred to 1 Service Flying Training School (India), K2090 was SOC in October 1942.

Harts were tough, many surviving accidents or forced landings that would have caused other types to be written off. Here K4483 is seen near the Beersheba to Jerusalem road after its engine quit on 1 November 1937 while operating with Ismailia-based 6 Squadron whose motif (visible on the fin) consisted of an eagle preying on a serpent, the latter loosely forming the numeral '6'. Repaired, K4483 was allocated to the Royal Egyptian Air Force on 16 March 1939.

While large numbers of Harts were ultimately modified to undertake new leases of life in various training roles, hundreds more were ordered as Hart Trainers from the outset, particularly in 1935/36, reflecting the increasing tempo of the RAF expansion schemes. Hart Trainer K5861 '25' was in the hands of 7 FTS when this photo was taken between October 1939 and January 1941. K5861 went on to serve with other flying schools, a glider pilot unit and lastly the Air Transport Auxiliary before being SOC on 24 January 1944. More than 500 Harts remained on the RAF books in September 1939; this after 230 or so had been transferred to the SAAF in 1938, to say nothing of the numbers that must have been written off since 1930.

A variant of the Hart, the Hawker Audax was developed for army co-operation duties and, externally at least, could be distinguished from the Hart by virtue of the hinged message-retrieving hook (if fitted) which was attached to the undercarriage axle. The first Audax unit was Farnborough-based 4 Squadron which began receiving the type in December 1931. Audax K4842, seen here, had been issued to India-based 20 Squadron at Peshawar (modern-day Pakistan) by November 1937 and coded 'K'. Later changed to 'D', the code was amended to 'HN-D' when war commenced. K4842 was SOC at Peshawar on 24 April 1940. Approximately 400 Audaxes remained in service at home and abroad in September 1939, the last expiring sometime in 1944. (*Newark Air Museum*)

A number of Hawker Demons remained airworthy in September 1939, many of which were adapted for target towing duties and painted black and yellow for obvious reasons. While several Demons soldiered on, this one, K2857, was reduced to maintenance airframe status in March 1940 as 1853M.

Essentially an Audax, the Hardy was intended as a general duties machine fitted with 'doughnut' heavy-duty tyres for landing on rough ground and carried under-wing racks for supply containers or a variety of bombs. Just forty-seven production airframes were produced, all by Gloster Aircraft, the first going to 30 Squadron in April 1935, followed by 6 Squadron in early 1938. This photo of K4050, the first production Hardy, was taken in the UK. Later allocated to 30 Squadron followed by a period in reserve, K4050 was subsequently assigned to the Southern Rhodesian Air Force and was SOC in March 1941.

From late 1938, 6 Squadron's Hardys were coded 'ZD', changing to 'JV' in September 1939, at which time the Palestine-based unit had thirty or more Hardys to hand supplemented by Gauntlet I/IIs and Lysander Is. All were replaced by Lysander IIs between February and April 1940. Camouflaged but sadly unidentified, this Hardy displays its 'doughnut' tyres and message-retrieving hook to good effect.

The final Hart-inspired biplane to enter production, the Hawker Hector, was developed as an army co-operation aircraft to replace the Audax. Hectors were made recognizable by their Napier Dagger engines fitted in lieu of the ubiquitous Kestrel; the latter being required to power a large number of Hinds ordered as interim bombers under the expansion schemes. The Hector, as with all its Hart-related forebears (aside from the Demon), carried the same First World War armament of one fixed and one flexible .303 machine gun. Excluding prototype K3719, 178 Hectors were produced commencing with K8090, which flew in February 1937. The Hectors shown here belonged to 614 Squadron, an army co-operation unit, and were photographed between 9 September 1938 (when K9766 joined the unit) and 18 July 1939 (when K9762 left). However, the lack of camouflage suggests that this image dates from September 1938. (*Newark Air Museum*)

Despite having been folded across its middle, this damaged photograph is interesting in that it shows camouflaged Hector K8104 'in action', with a note on the reverse advising that it was probably taken while operating against German forces near Calais on 26 May 1940. In fact, Hectors from 613 Squadron *did* deploy to RAF Lympne and *did* dive-bomb German field gun emplacements near Calais on that day using 120lb bombs, then returned the next day to drop supplies to beleaguered British troops in Calais. Sadly, from this caption's perspective, K8104 was with 612 (army co-operation) Squadron when this photo was taken and remained so until 28 May 1939 when it crashed near Dyce and was written off!

Hawker Henley K5115. The Henley was designed as a two-seat light day-bomber armed with a fixed Vickers machine gun, one flexibly-mounted Lewis gun and 550lb of bombs. Powered by a Merlin engine and utilizing several Hurricane I components, Henleys went into production but never into operational service, most being relegated to gunnery schools and anti-aircraft training units as target tugs. K5115 made its first flight in March 1937 and was SOC in May 1941. (*Tony Buttler collection*)

Henley L3243, the first of 200 production airframes, seen here in late 1938 or early 1939. For whatever reason, the Air Ministry changed its mind about light bomber requirements, which did nothing to prevent the later slaughter of Fairey Battles over the Low Countries in 1940. Speculation subsequently arose as to why the better-performing Henley had been sidelined, although the answer was apparently sidelined too. One thing is certain, however: even though the Henley's performance was better than a Battle, the difference between the two could never have been sufficient to save them from German anti-aircraft batteries, let alone the Bf 109E! (*Tony Buttler collection*)

The Vickers Valentia was a bulbous open-cockpit transport developed from the earlier Victoria V. Indeed, many were conversions from the earlier type and as a consequence their serial numbers were altered by adding the letter 'R', thus Victoria V K1313 became Valentia KR1313. Valentias were long-lived with some surviving into 1944, although K4635, seen here, was less fortunate. Allocated to Drigh Road, India (now in Pakistan), it joined the BTF (Bomber-Transport Flight) in September 1935 coded 'C' and remained with the BTF until it was absorbed by 31 Squadron in April 1939. Unfortunately, while taking off at Risalpur on 27 August 1939, both engines failed and K4635 struck a building, leaving it damaged beyond repair. Valentias benefitted from having a nose hatch that allowed stretchers and larger items of cargo to be passed beneath the cockpit into the fuselage.

Commencing life as Victoria V K2801 in 1932, this airframe was later converted to become Valentia KR2801 in 1934/35 by Vickers. Assigned to 70 Squadron in Iraq in 1936, it was allocated to the SAAF on 19 March 1940 and re-serialed as 265. Generally used as transports, Valentias could carry up to 2,200lb of bombs on under-wing racks, with some having ad hoc dorsal and fuselage gun positions fitted for self-defence.

Completed in February 1932, Vickers Vildebeest I S1715 was apparently unique inasmuch as it was completed as a night-bomber and allocated to 7 Squadron on 11 July 1933 for service trials. Its camouflage scheme was probably a very dark grey-green colour known as NIVO (night invisible varnish, Orfordness), a colour generally applied to British night-bombers from about 1917. Presumably the type proved unsuccessful as a night-bomber and was rejected. S1715 was later sent to the A&AEE for use in a series of trials until, while landing at RAF Orfordness, it hit a concrete block sometime in 1938 and didn't fly again.

Vildebeest II K2939 was delivered new to 100 Squadron at Seletar, Singapore in February 1934 where it was coded '3'. Subsequently transferred to the Kai Tak Station Flight at Hong Kong, K2939 came to grief there and was SOC in May 1939. The 'gun' in the rear cockpit appears to be a wind-operated winch, its rotor and arm having been pivoted through 90 degrees to reduce drag.

The Vickers Vincent was developed from the Vildebeest to provide the RAF with a general-purpose aircraft to replace the ageing Wapiti and Fairey IIIF abroad. Vildebeest I S1714 became the Vincent prototype and is seen here undergoing service trials in the Middle East in 1932/33. Later transferred to India, S1714 crashed at Kohat in February 1935 and was SOC. The principal feature distinguishing a Vincent from a Vildebeest was the long-range tank carried in lieu of a torpedo; otherwise the two were virtually identical. (*Newark Air Museum*)

An unidentified Vincent displays its long-range tank and message pick-up hook, fixed fuselage-mounted Vickers gun and rear-firing Lewis gun; they could also carry a 1,100lb bomb load. Vincents were tough and were used to carry out bombing operations against Italian forces in the Middle East and East Africa, often working from rough airstrips well into 1942. Thereafter, survivors continued to provide valuable service in subsidiary roles. (*Newark Air Museum*)

Vincent K6363 served with 244 Squadron from November 1940 until January 1943, a period in which the unit operated variously from Iraq and Oman. In mid-1942, the Air Ministry introduced newly-proportioned national markings, thus conveniently providing an approximate date for this otherwise undated photo, the inclusion of which again emphasizes the longevity of RAF biplanes as opposed to the introduction of ex-naval biplanes such as the Albacore, Swordfish and Walrus. K6363 was later allocated to the Anti-Locust Flight (Persia) at Bandar Abbas, and was finally SOC on 27 July 1944. (*Tony O'Toole collection*)

The Westland Lysander was developed as a two-seat replacement for the Audax and Hector. Powered by a Bristol Mercury engine, the high-wing monoplane could carry a Browning .303 in each wheel spat to which stub wings could also be fitted to carry small supply containers or light bombs. One, later two, hand-held machine guns were supplied for the observer. Lysander K6127, the first prototype, made its initial flight on 15 June 1935. It was this machine that was later transformed into a tandem-wing, twin-fin aircraft with a mock four-gun turret in the tail. Later used for all manner of experiments, K6127 was eventually SOC on 13 June 1944. (*Newark Air Museum*)

The second Lysander prototype, K6128, flew for the first time on 11 December 1936, and following performance trials in the UK was despatched to India in February 1938 to undertake tropical and service trials. K6128 became a ground instruction airframe in July 1940. (*Newark Air Museum*)

Lysander II L4759, complete with stub wings, was delivered new to 13 Squadron, an army co-operation unit, in early 1939. The six-pointed star on the fin denotes a reconnaissance unit which likely contains the Squadron motif - a lynx's head in front of a dagger. L4759 was SOC on 30 July 1940. (*Carl Vincent via Tony O'Toole*)

A fitter works on Lysander II R1999's Bristol Perseus XII engine in 1940. 'LX-P', a 225 Squadron machine, was fitted with stub wings and a loaded Vickers 'K' machine gun for the observer complete with a bag to catch spent .303 cartridge casings. R1999 went on to serve with 241 Squadron and 8 AACU before being SOC in August 1943. (*Newark Air Museum*)

As previously recorded, the Westland Wapiti served operationally at home with auxiliary squadrons until the last were withdrawn in January 1937, although the type remained operational in the Middle East and India for a while longer. Here India-based Wapiti IIA J9397 – unit unknown – accompanies 11 Squadron Hart 'K2126' (remember K1418, the one with the replacement rudder?) in the 1930s. J9397 was SOC on 6 July 1936.

Wapiti IIAs in formation over Iraq in the early 1930s. Belonging to 55 Squadron and based at RAF Hinaidi, Iraq from 1924 to September 1937, Wapitis were used by the unit from 1930 to March 1937, when Vincents replaced them. This image pre-dates November 1933, the month that J9631 'C1' was transferred to 84 Squadron. All three display the unit's motif on their fins. The wording in the curved scroll reads '*Nil nos tremefacit*' ('Nothing shakes us'), above which is the number '55' and above that a forearm with hand grasps a spear. (*Newark Air Museum*)

Based at Kohat on the North-West Frontier from late 1928 to 1939, 27 Squadron's ageing DH.9As were replaced in 1930 by the Wapiti, an aircraft made up of as many DH.9A components as possible in the interests of economy. Here Wapiti IIA K1291 'F', carrying a full bomb load beneath wings and fuselage, was also fitted for army co-operation duties as indicated by the letters 'AC' on the aft fuselage. Interestingly, the Squadron's elephant motif on the fin faces forward, while on others the starboard motif faced aft. Further, the motif itself sits within the frame of a 'grenade', indicating a bomber squadron, whereas army co-operation units used a six-pointed star – if applied at all. (See caption for Gauntlet K5359 regarding 'role-related frames'). Ultimately, this image conveys something of the true value of a general-purpose aircraft during the inter-war period; namely, rugged utility irrespective of any role markings carried. K1291's service history is vague, but we do know that in early 1942 it was with 5 Flight, Indian Air Force, at Cochin where it was SOC in January 1943. (*Newark Air Museum*)

An unidentified army co-operation Wapiti V, complete with message pick-up hook, making an atmospheric take-off. Thirty-five Mk Vs were built for service in India where the majority of surviving RAF Wapitis were based when the Second World War commenced. Most were quickly allocated to the Indian Air Force who used them into 1943. Perhaps the last service examples, however, were those used by the RCAF who operated the Wapiti IIA in a support role until as late as 1944.

The Westland Wallace, previously mentioned in the bomber section, found useful employment in several lesser roles once their replacement by Hart and Hind light bombers commenced in 1936. Ordinarily the Wallace would have been quietly phased out of service, but by 1936 the expansion schemes ensured they would survive for a bit longer. This image shows ex-Wapiti IIA K1346 at Yeovil following its 1932/33 conversion by Westland to become the first production Wallace I. Having received a new serial number, K3562 went on to serve with several units prior to being SOC in June 1942.

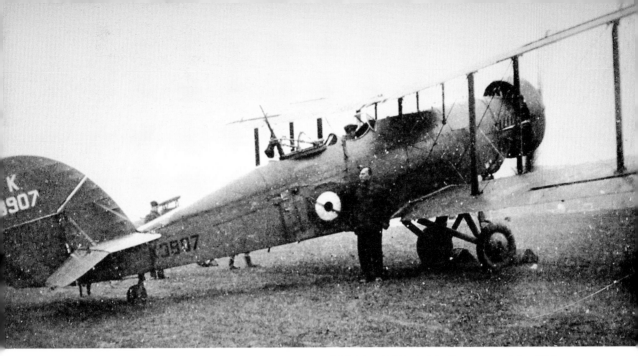

This grainy image, taken in 1939, shows Wallace I K3907 in 1939. Originally operated by 504 Squadron from March 1934 until mid-1937, K3907 was subsequently used by various Air Observer Schools and remained in use until February 1940 when it became ground instructional airframe 1813M. Approximately forty Wallace Is and about eighty Wallace IIs remained available to the RAF in September 1939.

Belonging to the Gunnery Research Unit which had formed at Exeter on 3 June 1940, Wallace I K4344 'HP-K' was photographed two years later while in use as a target tug; note the wind-operated winch and rotor (pivoted through 90 degrees) between the two cockpits. Originally constructed as Wapiti IIA K2313, it was returned to Westland in June 1934 and reconstructed as Wallace K4344. It was finally SOC in August 1943.

K6012 was an early Wallace II, a mark which introduced an enclosed canopy for both crew members, its rear section providing a distinctive 'lobster-back' appearance that covered the observer/rear gunner. K6012 became 943M following a collision with a plough in fog on 19 September 1936.

A closer view of the somewhat intricate Wallace II cockpit canopy.

Chapter Five

**Waiting in the Wings:
The New Order(s)**

It isn't always appreciated that when Britain went to war some of the aircraft destined to enter operational service in 1941 had already flown in prototype form in 1939, or at least would soon do so. Some would be successful with names familiar to the British public and the enemy, albeit for different reasons! Others were rather less so. Presented alphabetically by manufacturer, this final segment offers a glimpse of some of the types under development by late 1939.

L7247, the second prototype Avro Manchester, flew for the first time on 26 May 1940, ten months after the first prototype, L7246, on 25 July 1939. Flight trials with L7246 revealed from the outset that the Rolls-Royce Vulture engine was unable to produce sufficient power, was unreliable and likely to either fail entirely or catch fire in flight. It was a failure and production ceased after just over 500 examples had been produced, Manchesters being the main recipients. Nevertheless, the exigencies of the day ensured that the type would enter operational service, thus Waddington-based 207 Squadron became the first (of an eventual seven) to receive them in November 1940. Here, L7247 displays its small shark-like central fin fitted to counteract a degree of lateral instability encountered during L7246's flight trials, as well as its FN21A two-gun ventral turret seen lowered for the camera. (*Tony Buttler collection*)

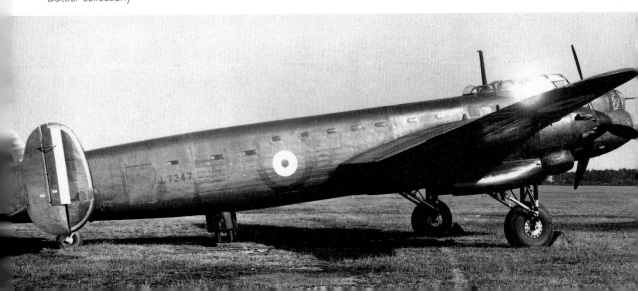

Here, L7247's ventral turret is retracted while its original central fin has been replaced by one of new design. Seen from this angle, L7247 provides more than a hint of how the Manchester's eventual successor would look. Both L7246 and L7247 survived to become ground instructional airframes in November 1942 and October 1941 respectively. (*Tony Buttler collection*)

Designed to meet the requirements for a reconnaissance flying boat, the Blackburn B.20 uniquely incorporated a planing bottom that retracted to meet the upper fuselage once the airframe and propeller tips were clear of the water, while its wing floats, retracting outwards, folded neatly into the underside of each wing to form elongated wing tips. B.20, serial number V8914, flew for the first time on 26 March 1940 but sadly crashed a few days later into the Firth of Clyde on 7 April, apparently as a result of aileron flutter. Powered by two Vulture engines, the B.20 had a span of 82ft 2in and was reportedly credited with a maximum speed of 306 mph. Although the retractable lower hull concept was vindicated, further development of the B.20 ceased.

Designed as a heavily-armed long-range fighter utilizing various Beaufort components for ease of production, the two-seat Bristol Beaufighter became one of the Second World War's famous aircraft. Powerful and versatile, it would add the roles of night-fighter, fighter-bomber and torpedo-bomber to its repertoire plus, towards the end of its life, that of target tug as well, a duty the Beaufighter TT.10 performed until the last examples were grounded in 1960. (*Tony Buttler collection*)

From the outset, as these photos of first prototype R2052 testify, the Beaufighter projected a sense of robust strength and power, an image enhanced by the snub-nosed cockpit, Bristol Hercules radial engines and, on production airframes, four 20mm Hispano cannon and six Browning .303 machine guns. R2052 made its maiden flight on 17 July 1939 and survived until damaged beyond repair on 23 February 1941. (*Tony Buttler collection*)

Handley Page Halifax L7244, the first prototype Halifax, made its maiden flight on 25 October 1939. One assumes that this photo dates from approximately that time. (*Tony Buttler collection*)

Halifax L7245, the second prototype, was first flown on 17 August 1940 with power-operated turrets fitted fore and aft. Both prototypes were powered by Merlin engines, as were production Halifax Mks I, II and V, none of which enjoyed a particularly outstanding reputation, made worse by Bomber Command chief Arthur 'Bomber' Harris, who severely criticized the Halifax and wanted an all-Lancaster force. Opinions would change significantly, however, following the later introduction of the Mks III and VI. They transformed the Halifax by introducing Hercules engines as well as significant improvements to the airframe, both internal and external. Harris, nevertheless, remained unimpressed! Both prototypes survived to be relegated to ground instructional airframe status in 1942. (*Tony Buttler collection*)

The prototype Short Stirling, L7600, made its maiden flight on 14 May 1939 and although the flight went well the landing didn't, with L7600 being written off after its undercarriage collapsed; a severe impediment to the bomber's development schedule. Undeterred, the company's second prototype, L7605, flew on 24 December 1939 and development continued. This image shows the first production Stirling, N3635, which made its first flight on 7 May 1940. Used for research and development purposes, N3635 was damaged beyond repair at Boscombe Down when it swung during a rocket-assisted take-off on 16 August 1941. (*Tony Buttler collection*)

The Westland Whirlwind became the first twin-engined single-seat fighter to enter RAF service. Powered by two liquid-cooled 885hp Rolls-Royce Peregrine engines, Whirlwinds could achieve 360 mph at 15,000ft and were armed with four fixed 20mm cannon in the nose with sixty rounds per gun. Service introduction began in July 1940 with 263 Squadron, with others going to 137 Squadron from February 1941. Ultimately only 112 production Whirlwinds were built and the type remained in service until late 1943. This image shows prototype Whirlwind L6844, painted very dark grey or black overall, possibly on the occasion of its first flight on 11 October 1938. Used by the RAE, A&AEE and the Air Fighting Development Unit among others, L6844 became ground instructional airframe 3063M in April 1942.